# Gardens for the Future

# Gardens for the Future

Gestures Against the Wild

Guy Cooper and Gordon Taylor

THE MONACELLI PRESS

# Contents

## Case Studies

**Page 1** Filigreed Line, *1979, a plasma-cut aluminum sculpture that was site-generated from the landscape at Wellesley College in Massachusetts by Robert Irwin.*

**Title page** *This painted, welded steel sculpture is one of three "garden follies" made by Thomas Balsley for a public park called Gate City in Osaki, Tokyo, Japan. This piece, made in 1998, was inspired by sedge leaves. It is entitled* Carex.

**Far left, top** *Sculptural ocotillo stems* (Fouquieria splendens) *in the Arizona desert.*

**Far left, bottom** *Part of a fabulous water feature in the grounds of the headquarters of the Banque Générale du Luxembourg, Plateau de Kirchberg, on the edge of the city.*

**Above** *Palm oasis for "The Citadel," Commerce, California.*

**Left** *These angular walls in a private garden in Phoenix, Arizona, were inspired by Alvar Aalto.*

# Introduction

In 1996, we published *Paradise Transformed*, our first book on the subject of garden and landscape design at the end of the millennium. Although it is now considered one of the first major popular books on contemporary landscape, its publication did not mark an end to our obsessive pursuit of the subject. *Gardens for the Future: Gestures Against the Wild* represents a second phase in our compulsive journey toward some definition of private gardens and public landscapes at the end of the twentieth century. It also embraces developments in the use of materials and the principles of design that have occurred since the first book was written.

We are not cultural commentators or pundits. This is a personal selection, and as such it cannot be totally comprehensive. We have tried to avoid the private language of academic landscape design. However, we have adopted the three definitions of landscape coined by Robert Irwin, the visionary American artist. Irwin refers to landscape or garden designs as being either site dominant, site adjusted, or site generated. As we make extensive use of these terms ourselves, it is important that their meaning should be clear.

Site-dominant gardens have no real place in a book about contemporary design. Irwin used the term to refer to the highly influential gardens of sixteenth-century Italy, seventeenth-century France, and eighteenth-century England. These are gardens that have become historical models. They are relevant to our theme only as sources of inspiration for contemporary designers.

Site-adjusted gardens draw their inspiration from a multitude of sources. In this respect the site-dominant landscapes and gardens are very important. In our Age of Information, however, the field of reference can range from ancient labyrinths to the electro-diode light sculpture installations of the avant-garde.

The second part of this book consists of twenty case studies of private and public landscapes that illustrate the incredible diversity of achievement at the end of the twentieth century. Of these studies, thirteen are site-adjusted designs. They include Jacques Wirtz's garden in the Tuileries in Paris, which draws inspiration from European garden history, as do the designs of Daniel Urban Kiley in the United States and Femando Caruncho in Spain and Florida. Ton ter Linden in Holland was influenced by the large-scale use of herbaceous perennials in early-twentieth-century Germany. Other case studies reflect the influences of China and Japan.

We were amused by the notion that British gardens of the eighteenth century could be simultaneously defined as both site dominant and site adjusted. They were inspired by an enormous wave of Italian influence on art, architecture, and the landscape at that time, which makes them site adjusted. However, over the past three hundred years, the classical gardens of eighteenth-century Britain have become so closely identified with the British landscape that they are now historical models within the context of Britain's cultural history and can now be read as site dominant.

It has emerged from our research that some of the most important gardens and landscapes of the past twenty years have been site generated. In simple terms, these are designs inspired by the intrinsic nature of the site. The design forms are drawn both from

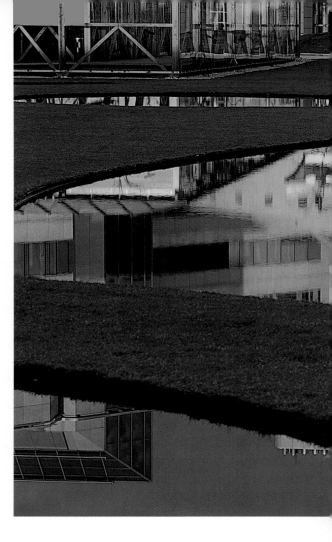

the physical features of the site and its surroundings and from information not visible to the naked eye, such as geology and history. These gardens and landscapes are the very antithesis of site-adjusted designs, since they evolve from the landscape rather than being imposed upon it.

Site-generated designs are a truly unique and innovative contribution to garden and landscape design in the late twentieth century. Although Alexander Pope's splendid admonition to "Consult the Genius of the Place in all" is often misquoted, the best and most exciting site-generated designs to have emerged can be seen as true, late-twentieth-century adaptations of Pope's wonderful command.

The post-industrial and postmodern realities of our time find their expression in site-generated landscape designs, which draw their inspiration from contemporary culture and the environment. They are intrinsic to our society, just as the site-dominant gardens of Villa d'Este, Vaux-le-Vicomte, or Stourhead were to theirs, and as such they are a true reflection of late-twentieth-century culture.

Site-generated garden and landscape designs seem to embody characteristics that could be defined as sense and sensibility. The "sense" is in the shapes that emerge from a deep analysis of the site. The "sensibility" is found in the aesthetic qualities resulting from this process. Every aspect of the site,

**Above** *The International Style headquarters of the Banque Générale du Luxembourg is set in a formal landscape designed by Jacques Wirtz. Here he has combined a serpentine lawn with water to offset the austerity of the building.*

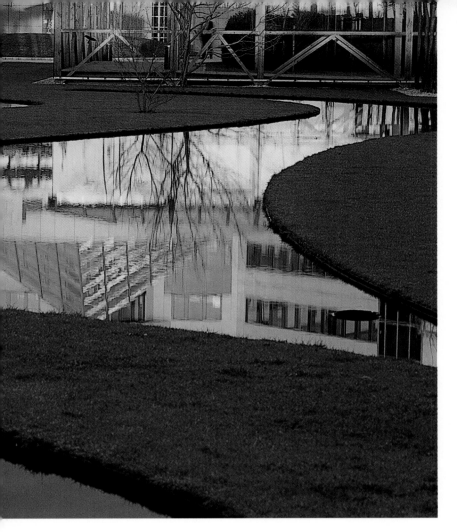

both visible and invisible, is taken into account and transformed into inspirational material.

Many site-generated landscapes are created on abandoned industrial land. The site itself must be thoroughly analyzed before the design process begins. An investigation of the history of the site is the first stage of this procedure. All visual information—including old engravings and views, sketches, and photomontages—is studied alongside any written material. This historical analysis will produce a rich pool of material that can be built into the design. It will also reveal a pattern of growth and change. The effects of the climatic conditions and the seasons are also recorded, as is the annual rainfall. The site is observed during both the day and night, and the soil is analyzed. This analysis includes the study of earth forms, soil textures and levels, existing drainage, and drainage needs. The exploratory work is usually carried out by a multidisciplinary, collaborative team, all pursuing the same objective.

Site-generated case studies in this book show the work of Robert Irwin, George Hargreaves, Mark Rios, Desvigne & Dalnoky, D.A.ST., Thomas Balsley, and Kathryn Gustafson.

Despite the diversity of their output, the designers represented here have a common aim. They are all in pursuit of innovation. We hope that you will find their gardens and landscapes as exciting and inspiring as we have.

**Below** Nine Spaces, Nine Trees, *Seattle, 1983.*
*Robert Irwin's site-generated philosophy*
*is a powerful force in landscape*
*design and architecture.*

# Cultural Influences

Landscapes are culture before they are nature; constructs of the imagination projected onto wood, water and rock.

Simon Schama

**Above** *A contemporary New Mexico garden with drought-resistant plants softening the concrete walls. The design may reflect the influence of sculptor Richard Serra.*

**Above right** *Glass gravel has been put to exquisite use in a private garden in Los Angeles, creating a beautiful ground cover of melding layers of crushed glass.*

Since the late 1930s, there has been a constant cross-fertilization in garden and landscape design between Europe, North and South America, and Japan. In these places, landscape design often reflects the influence of twentieth-century art—from Cubism to Minimalism—and architecture—from Bauhaus to the New York Five. Within this cultural context, three great twentieth-century artists and designers have had a very specific influence on the evolution of contemporary landscape. They are the Brazilian painter Roberto Burle Marx, the Japanese-American sculptor Isamu Noguchi, and the Mexican architect Luis Barragán. No college degrees in landscape architecture are needed after

these names. However, formally trained landscape architects have also made their impact. Thomas Church, Daniel Urban Kiley, Garrett Eckbo, James Rose, and Ian McHarg are some of the most important names to emerge since 1950. The combined effect of these diverse influences has been to inspire landscape designers and architects to think in terms of the twentieth century.

Historical styles are no longer embraced by modern designers as total models. The gardens that are created for our technological society draw their inspiration from contemporary architecture, art, and film and, wherever possible, from the site itself. Late-twentieth-century landscape design is extremely diverse. However, some salient characteristics can be identified. The first of these relates to the treatment of space. Contemporary designers have been inspired by modern art and architecture to think of space in three dimensions and to take a sculptural approach to its use. Gardens are no longer laid out in the traditional manner along a single axis. The notion of multi-axial, diagonal, and asymmetric spaces has been inherited by our designers from the Cubists. Abstract art has had an equally important influence in design, which is reflected in curvilinear and biomorphic shapes found in the garden. Finally, and by way of contrast, geometric and rectilinear forms have been drawn from the International Style of architecture and used in contemporary garden design.

Not all of the traditional spatial models have been rejected. For example, the *ur*-Islamic layout—the most traditional mode of garden design known to Western civilization—marries well with the rectilinear style of twentieth-century architecture, creating a closer integration of the house and garden.

The work of contemporary designers has resulted in a greater emphasis on gardens as places for people. Designers have to confront social issues and the changes in social structures and working patterns.

Some garden designers have even been asked to make nighttime gardens that can be used by shift workers. Others have learned how to create gardens in tiny niches which are part of the urban landscape, such as balconies, stairwells, and paved areas.

A greater awareness of ecology is also reflected in contemporary gardens. Modern designers are concerned with the ecological health of the site, and this concern is often reflected in the planting of native grasses and drought-resistant plants.

The sophisticated technology available at the end of the twentieth century has produced many new materials. Plastics, metals, fiberglass rock formations, fiber-optic lighting, and artificial fog began to be used in public landscapes at the beginning of the 1980s. Now they are starting to be seen in private gardens as well.

Diversity is the hallmark of contemporary design. Below is an alphabetical list that spans some of the many different influences upon landscape and garden design at the end of the twentieth century.

**Abstract art** was one of the great contributive influences on all of the arts in the twentieth century. Since the 1950s, some of the earliest roots for landscape architecture have been variations on either the geometric or the hard-edge form of abstraction coined by Constructivists such as Malevich and Rodchenko; concrete art, practiced by Theo van Doesberg and Josef Albers; or the more relaxed, organic form of the abstract used by Hans Arp and Joan Miró and referred to as the biomorphic.

**Age of Information** Landscape architecture and design have started to benefit from new technology since the invention of CAD, computer-aided design. This is especially helpful with larger projects. Easy access to information about historic gardens and the gardens of other cultures has opened up a rich new seam of reference for the designers of site-adjusted gardens.

**Alvar Aalto** The great Finnish architect, designer, and artist was one of the most important architects of the modern movement and contributed greatly to garden

and landscape design. His combined treatment of house and garden, and his biomorphic shapes, were an inspiration to Thomas Church.

**Artificial fog** is another technological advance used by garden and landscape designers over the past twenty years. It is made by water being atomized under high pressure. The wonderful, mysterious effect this produces blurs landscape elements and boundaries instantly, lending a surreal otherworldliness to the design. Human-made fog has also been used in gardens in extremely hot climates for its cooling properties.

**Automobile** Clients often ask us to mask or reroute the car and its function in relation to the house and garden. The machine must be concealed and yet accessible. Has Filippo Marinetti's notion on modern life in the *Futurist Manifesto* finally become a reality with the automobile in 1999, "a life of steel, fever, pride and headlong speed"?

**Luis Barragán** The Mexican architect is one of the most significant modernist influences on contemporary landscape design. His square and rectangular planar wall shapes were inspired by Muslim tradition in Spain and Morocco and the architecture of Le Corbusier, the International Style, and the vernacular buildings of the Mediterranean and Mexico. Counterpointing his minimalist walls with simple pools, channels, and artificial waterfalls, Barragán developed an elegant and simple style that continues to influence landscape architects and designers throughout the world.

**Bauhaus** This important early-twentieth-century school of art and architecture in Dessau, Germany, was the font of modernism. After it was closed by the Nazis in the 1930s, many of the artists, architects, and teachers, including Walter Gropius, fled to the United States. Gropius became head of architecture at Harvard. His teaching contributed greatly to the development of landscape architecture in the United States after World War II.

**Roberto Burle Marx** was another primary influence on landscape architecture and design in the twentieth century. He trained as a painter and applied his artistic

*Above* The Plaza of the Japanese-American Cultural Center, Los Angeles, by Isamu Noguchi.

*Far right* One of many horse pools by Luis Barragán, Mexico's great modern architect; his planar colored stucco designs have influenced contemporary landscape architects all over the world.

**Right** *Cross-cultural inspiration on the Costa Cayeres in Mexico. Humankind's most ancient design, the labyrinth, has been used as a terrace around an invisible-edge swimming pool. In this case, the design was inspired by the nave floor of Chartres Cathedral.*

eye to his native Brazil. His trademark was the use of large-scale, free-flowing biomorphic drifts of indigenous native plants as exquisite ground cover. He loathed the word "style" and viewed each of his designs as a union between art and nature.

**Chain-link fencing** has abandoned its traditional role as a security barrier and begun to be used sculpturally in gardens and landscapes. Some years ago, when we first began to find out about the contemporary garden, we saw this material being used in the landscape and were not impressed. Years later, we understand that chain-link fencing has great value as a late-twentieth-century material.

**Circle** Along with the spiral, serpentine, and zigzag, the circle is one of the most primitive marks made by humankind and has been used in endless variations over many millennia. Today these shapes are being used once more in their pure form by contemporary landscape designers.

**Conceptual art** was a phrase used by the artist Sol Lewitt in the late 1960s to refer to works of art in which the idea rather than the object is most important. Its roots go back to the art of Ready-mades by Marcel Duchamp, one of the most influential artists of the twentieth century. Other important figures are Yves Klein and Piero Manzoni. Video and performance art were spin-offs. In the landscape, the most inspirational form of conceptual art is earth or land art.

**Cubism** The name of this important modern art movement arose when a French art critic heard Matisse refer to a painting by Braque as just some "little cubes." Picasso and Braque were the first Cubists, and they changed the use of perspective that had been primary to painting since the Renaissance. In landscape design this translates into abstraction and the creation of simultaneous points of view, which was used first by a few French designers in some gardens and landscapes in the 1920s—Robert Mallet-Stevens, André and Paul Vera, and Gabriel Guevrekian. From the 1950s on, American landscape architects such as Garrett Eckbo, James Rose, and Thomas Church were all influenced by it.

**Dada** Topher Delaney and Martha Schwartz are two American landscape designers who often speak of the influence of Dada on their work. Provocation, humor, and absurdity were Dada characteristics. Marcel Duchamp would probably have approved of Delaney's Garden of Divorce and Schwartz's Bagel Garden.

**Drought resistance** During the past thirty years, there has been among landscape architects and designers a heightened awareness of the need to consider ecology and the environment. During the last fifteen years, the prospect of increased global warming has emerged. This is allied to important

issues of resource sustainability: supplies of water that had been taken for granted for centuries must now be husbanded more sensibly and efficiently. Plants from more arid habitats are becoming popular and are being used in garden and landscape designs in many countries of the world—even in northern temperate areas where rainfall can be optimum.

**Ecological awareness** In the early decades of the twentieth century, Jens Jensen was voicing his concern about the environment in relation to landscape design. Subsequently, many prominent thinkers and landscape designers have become involved in the ecological debate. At the beginning of the 1960s, Ian McHarg led the field. Since the 1970s it has been Richard Oehme and James van Sweden in the United States and Ton ter Linden, Piet Oudolf, and Hank Geritsen in Holland who have made great contributions to the ecological discussion. Naturalistic plantings of varying heights characterize this style. Leaf shapes and textures create structural contrasts, and there is an emphasis on grasses, the beauty of spent plants in the fall and winter, and planting that requires low maintenance.

**Energy conservation** Allied to ecological awareness is an attempt by the profession to factor energy conservation and sustainable resources into designs for both gardens and landscapes. Reconstituted stone is used for paving, outdoor composition board takes the place of natural wood for carpentry features, retention pond systems gather run-off water for use in the landscape, and "gray" recycled water is used for water incidents. Solar-powered pumps provide the energy to drive small water features, and low-voltage/high-intensity outdoor lighting systems are used.

**Fiberglass** This inexpensive, flexible, tough, weather-resistant material is being used more and more in gardens and landscapes to make hard architectural landscape features, completely natural-looking stones and boulders in myriad shapes, sculptures, paving slabs, and sections for walls.

*Below Sand-blasted glass-panel walls are up-lit by white neon to make a mysterious and elegant enclosure for a terrace in San Francisco. The evergreen grass stripes are Dichondra miscantha.*

**Fiber optics** have been transforming garden and landscape lighting since the 1980s. The technology came out of research for telecommunications and medical practice. The low-voltage, high-intensity lighting is extremely flexible and can be housed in a huge variety of cabling, both clear and opaque. Any element of the garden or landscape can be lit by the use of fiber optics.

**Fibonacci sequence** This was developed by Leonardo of Pisa in 1202, and it is one of the earliest mathematical models. Out of the sequence, each term from 3 on is the sum of the previous two. For example, 55 = 34 + 21. The same elegant sequence of numbers is found in the petal, sepal, stamen, and seedhead conformations of many plants. Some designers in the United States and Japan have used the sequence in the scale and proportion of the elements in designs.

**Glass** Advances in glass technology over the past two decades have made many forms of glass available to landscape architects and designers. Glass comes in many specifications: toughened, double skinned, and even ground up and used as gravel. It is also beginning to be used as an alternative to the endless machine-made terra cotta of recent years.

**Global warming** Awareness of this phenomenon has emerged over the past twenty years, and the more ecologically minded landscape architects and designers have tried to factor this atmospheric negative into their work. Northern climes can now take more drought-resistant plants, for the weather is much warmer.

**Green architecture** Grass-roof technology; turf-covered underground houses in Denmark, Germany, and Mexico; solar-powered pumps for small ponds; houses made of hay: all these and more are examples of green architecture. Designs incorporating trees within architecture are being created by American and French landscape architects; James Wines of SITE and Edouard François have been at the forefront of this work.

**High-tech** Every aspect of our lives has been changed by the fax and e-mail, and digital everything is on its way. In landscape and garden design, fiber-optic

*__Left__ Overlapping sections of perforated steel provide security for the parking area in a Phoenix garden. On a sunny day the wall is semitransparent, creating a moiré effect. On a cloudy day it is opaque.*

*__Below__ The roof terrace of a multinational bank has brightly colored polymer-material benches, silk wind socks, and giant balls of ivy: a view to cheer up the computer operators inside the building. At night the terrace is lit so it can be appreciated by the night-shift workers.*

**Above** *A late-twentieth-century design for a courtyard in Santa Fe, New Mexico. The sound made by the falling water in this Islamic-style garden is increased by the metal linings of the raised pools.*

lighting, artificial fog, and videos as part of garden design (the Video Garden at the Massachusetts Institute of Technology) are part of this revolution.

**Kitsch** An extremely conservative traditional landscape designer from the Deep South of the United States reckons some avant-garde American landscape and garden designers in the late twentieth century have this trait. He sums up their work as ephemeral "one-liners" with the following: "Once you've seen a dog wearing lipstick, what else is there?"

**Land art,** or earth art, has had a significant influence on landscape architects and designers. The primary work in the mid-1960s was by many artists disenchanted with abstraction in both painting and sculpture. They also rejected the gallery/curator/critic

hype machine and were aware of the environmental movement. This position drew them to the endless sky and earth of the desert and non-arable wide open spaces of the western United States. Here the earth artists sculpted vast quantities of earth, often in shapes reminiscent of our ancient forebears' burial mounds and stone structures.

**Le Corbusier** Along with Mies van der Rohe, Le Corbusier was the leading proponent of the most influential twentieth-century architecture, the white rectilinear International Style. His visionary approach was not without its downside: under his influence, vertical slums were built all over the world after World War II, and many are now being demolished. Some great single elitist compositions—the chapel at

United States: Donald Judd, Sol Lewitt, Agnes Martin, Robert Morris, Richard Serra, and David Smith were some of its leading lights. Their ground-zero minimalist forms, lines, and groups of the same abstract geometric shapes set in seriality, cross-fertilized with the work of late-twentieth-century garden and landscape architects and designers, particularly in the work of Peter Walker.

**Neon** This wonderful, flexible, and relatively inexpensive twentieth-century design element has gone from billboards to signposting, and then to museum art installations. In the past twenty years it has found its way into the garden and landscape. Ian Hamilton Finlay, the great British poet and designer, was one of the first to use neon art installations. Adventurous landscape designers, particularly in the United States and Japan, have been including it in their designs.

**Isamu Noguchi** The important Japanese-American sculptor has had a significant influence on gardens and landscapes since the 1980s. His symbolic, sculptural garden and landscape designs included memorials, play parks, and bridges. Noguchi's use of stone, water, and a minimum of plants is seen in his masterpieces: Chase Manhattan Bank, New York City; Beinecke Rare Book and Manuscript Library, Yale University; and *California Scenario*, Costa Mesa, California.

**Plastics and polymers** are twentieth-century materials that are now finding their way into contem-

**Above** *A flower and vegetable patch designed for a plant-obsessed client in Paradise Valley, Arizona. The plants were all waiting in readiness for the garden to be completed.*

Ronchamp in eastern France and his Villa Savoye west of Paris (the last exemplified his view of the landscape with his white architecture set in a rural picturesque landscape)—alone would have secured his place in the history of twentieth-century architecture.

**Low maintenance** Landscape architects and designers have been asked, even told, to include this most important basic given in their designs. Evergreens are used in place of deciduous plants, to reduce the need for dead-leaf collecting. Groundcover plants are also widely used, to suppress weed growth. Technological development since the 1980s has meant that computers and sensors can control irrigation and lighting.

**Minimalism** is thought to have been the first modernist art movement to have emerged in the

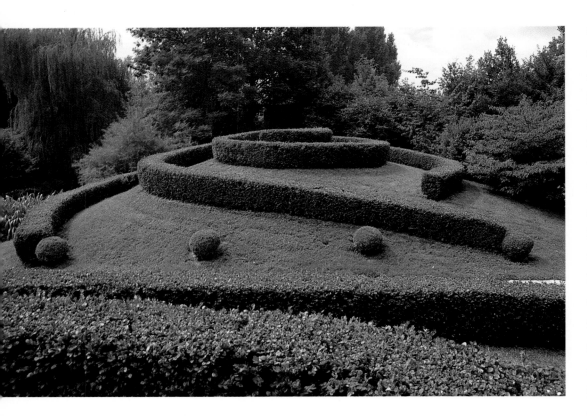

worldwide. Landscape design in Scandinavia incorporates the principles of social democracy and modern art. Sven-Ingar Andersson, the greatest living Danish landscape architect, says that "The very essence of our profession lies in the combination of design and architecture with ecology. "

**The serpentine** is an ancient form used as a contrast to the square or rectilinear. The designs of Sven-Ingar Andersson of Denmark and Ted Smyth of New Zealand provide wonderful examples.

**Site adjusted** is a term applied to landscape design by Robert Irwin in the United States and is used to define gardens and landscapes with a design that is influenced by the gardens of other cultures or periods.

**Site dominant** is another term used by Irwin. In this case it refers to the actual historical models from garden history, rather than to the gardens that they inspired.

**Site generated** is a term used by Irwin to define gardens with a design that has evolved from the intrinsic characteristics of the site.

**Spiral** This eternal form is seen in the spiral star galaxies, DNA, the double spiral of flowerets in the sunflower, and the household screw. It is used internationally in the designs of many renowned landscape

*Above* Spiral to Heaven *made from lawn and boxwood in a garden near Caen in Normandy, France.*

*Right* Mirror Trail, *Ithaca, New York, was made in 1969 by Robert Smithson. The effect of the snow is heightened and transformed by the use of mirrors and glass.*

porary gardens and landscapes in many different forms and configurations, such as perimeter fencing, retaining walls, paving, garden furniture, and sculpture.

**Postmodernism** This term is thought to have appeared first in *Architecture and the Spirit of Man* by Joseph Hudnut, 1949, but it was popularized by Charles Jencks in the late 1960s and given form in the architecture of Philip Johnson, Michael Graves, Robert Venturi, and others. It is a highly complex cluster of cultural ideas and phenomena. Just as there was a relationship between modernism and the industrialization of society, so there is between postmodernism and our contemporary, high-tech society. Postmodernism is a reaction against the spare, minimalist style of modernism. It is a hybrid, full of cultural references, and its forms are ambiguous. Garden and landscape designers like George Hargreaves, Adriaan Geuze, Kathryn Gustafson, and Desvigne & Dalnoky all have elements of the postmodern in their work.

**Scandinavian modern** is a major twentieth-century international design force. The Ant Chair by Jacobsen, Bang and Olufsen TV and music systems, and wind turbines are classic models from Denmark; Marimekko fabrics, Arabia pottery, and the designs of Alvar Aalto originated in Finland; Ikea of Sweden sells its products architects and designers: George Hargreaves's projects at Château de Chaumont near Tours, France, and the University of Cincinnati; the public park in Luxembourg with giant water retention ponds designed by the German designer Peter Latz; and the projected public park Abandoibarra by Balmori Associates in Bilbao, adjacent to the Guggenheim Museum, are but a few.

**Steels and metals**  Many types of steel have found their way into the late-twentieth-century landscape. Stainless steel and Cor-Ten are both commonly used to make retaining walls in gardens and landscapes. On a recent trip through Spain, we saw not only handsome cast-iron circular planters on ball feet but long, angular sheets of steel used as pavements in pedestrianized areas.

**Frank Lloyd Wright**  is considered the American master architect of the twentieth century and displayed enormous sensitivity toward the landscape in relation to his buildings: Fallingwater in Pennsylvania, Taliesin West, Arizona, and Hollyhock House, Los Angeles.

**Xeriscape**  "Xeri" means dry and is the current American buzzword for drought-resistant gardening techniques.

**Zigzag**  Along with the circle, spiral, and serpentine, this is one of humankind's most ancient marks or patterns, and it is used endlessly in garden and landscape design, from the pattern on the columns in the Treasury at Mycenae to the spirit bridges in Japanese gardens to the floor plan and fenestration pattern of the Jewish Museum in Berlin by Daniel Libeskind. The origin of the word itself is unknown. It is partly symbolic, for the two different vowels do suggest two different directions.

We see these influences reflected in a myriad of combinations in the gardens of the late twentieth century. George Hargreaves has his own view on where this new vocabulary of landscape architecture will lead:

> With this society's shift from belief in the new to its recognition of limits and interest in what exists, the stylistic explorations in postmodern landscape architecture have just begun. Time, nature, and culture will serve as physical media and subject. Light, shadow, sky, rain, plants, dirt, debris, people of all types, and man-made elements that intensify and abstract what is already here will become the focus of simpler, more receptive compositions and non-compositions. Where this will lead and what landscapes may come to look like is, of course, open-ended.

**Below**  *Fiber Wave is made from 150 carbon-fiber rods. It was created by the Japanese architect Makoto Wei Watanabe. He refers to it as "designless design," since the twelve-foot rods are moved randomly by the wind.*

New Functions

# Public Spaces

At the La Villette competition, we discovered the programmatic potential of landscape, and so I explained to [the late Yves Brunier] that, personally, I didn't find architecture particularly interesting, but that on the contrary, landscape represented an incredible potential.

Rem Koolhaas

**Above** *The main terrace of the Mondrian Hotel in Los Angeles designed by Philippe Starck. Nineteenth-century Victorian flowerpots have been scaled up to become giant, late-twentieth-century containers for multistemmed bay trees.*

**Previous pages** *Video image of the Pompidou Center, Paris, with a myriad of images in the Hanging Gardens of Golders Green, London.*

Adriaan Geuze, head of West 8, an important landscape design and architecture team based in Rotterdam, Holland, has this to say regarding public spaces:

> Green has become a kind of habit. And it has also become a cliché of its own . . . There is no need for parks anymore, because they have solved all the nineteenth-century problems and a new type of city has been created.

Despite these provocative words, the late twentieth century has brought an enormous diversity of design to gardens and landscapes used as public spaces.

During the early part of the nineteenth century, John Claudius Loudon and his wife, Jane, became the first crusaders for public parks in Great Britain. Loudon was one of the first Victorian garden visionaries to think about public parks in relation to the onslaught of the industrial revolution. He believed that such parks had the power to "raise the intellectual character of the lowest classes of society."

In the latter half of the nineteenth century, landscape design was largely dominated by the classical Beaux-Arts style. This prevailed until the late 1920s and the 1930s, which saw a radical change in the way that public spaces were designed. This change was a response to the influence of modernism and Le Corbusier. His white simple "machines for living" were surrounded by quasi-natural landscapes that usually consisted of a ground plane of grass punctuated by the vertical forms of trees.

Just before World War II, social need came to be seen as an important factor in the design of new buildings, gardens, and landscapes. Denmark was one of the leaders in this field. Here gardens and landscapes were designed around new public housing projects. This early Scandinavian "green" architecture became a source of inspiration for architects in postwar Europe and North America.

Sven-Ingar Andersson is described as the grand old man of Danish, if not Scandinavian, landscape architecture, and its greatest living designer. In his view, landscape design in twentieth-century Denmark has been based on social democratic principals allied to modern art. Klee, Kandinsky, Picasso, and Braque have all had an influence on Danish landscape design.

Andersson followed from G. N. Brandt and C. H. Sorenson, who were pioneers of landscape at the beginning of the twentieth century. It is a pity that few

*Below The Citadel, the former Uniroyal Tire and Rubber Company building, Commerce, California. Its facade is reminiscent of an Assyrian temple and was the inspiration for the oasis of palms planted there in 1991. The "ghosts of tires past" are made of concrete and used for sitting and for protecting the palms from cars.*

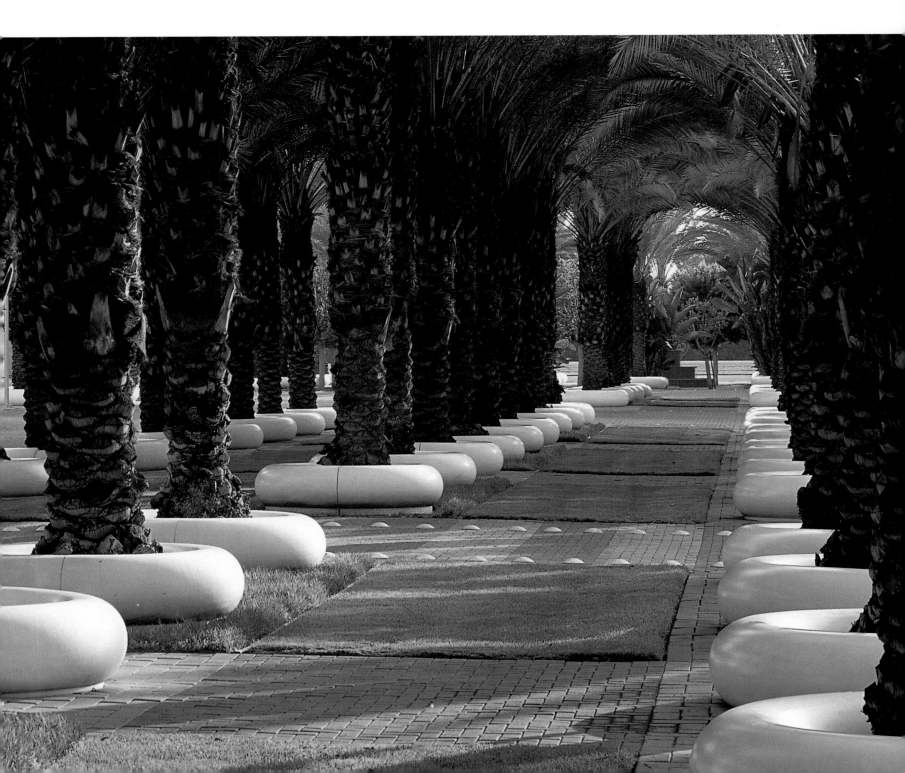

books in English exist on any of these visionary designers. Andersson credits Brandt and Sorenson with managing to combine Denmark's rural landscape with advancing urbanization and modern art. They were influenced by the use of the abstract that was displayed in modern architecture and painting. The public plazas and parks they built represent another layer of the Scandinavian modern style.

In the northern industrial countries, the last twenty or thirty years have seen a huge growth in garden and landscape spaces created for public use. The public park now has the highest profile in contemporary "place-making"—to quote Capability Brown, that great English designer of eighteenth-century landscapes. Many of Brown's picturesque landscapes have been

**Below** *One of twenty-six follies on grid points of the Parc de la Villette, the largest public park in Paris. Bernard Tschumi, the designer, described the design process in the following way: "First we decided that we were not going to be contextual . . . We were determined to literally start from a pure concept."*

amenities dates back to the 1870s in England.

There are many differences between the parks of the nineteenth century and those that belong to the twentieth. The four projects described here are intended to reflect the diversity of contemporary public spaces. One of the most striking contrasts between these parks and those of the nineteenth century is their location. Traditionally, the park was found in the center of a town or city. Today it can be situated anywhere, on the very edge of an urban area or some distance away from it.

## Parc de la Villette

Parc de la Villette was built in a Parisian suburb in the 1980s. The project represents another seismic shift in

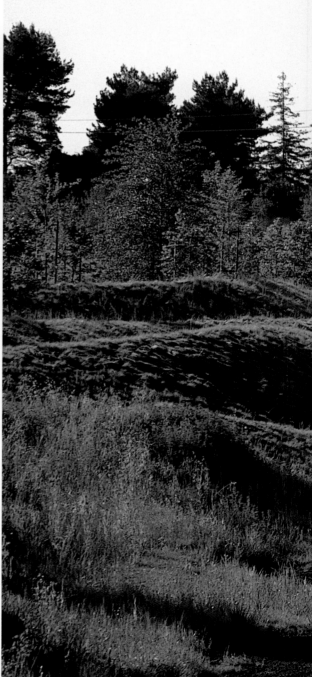

transformed into public parks since the end of World War II. Blenheim, Bowood, Chatsworth, Longleat, Petworth, and Weston Park: all these are now open.

It should be remembered, however, that public access is not an entirely modern concept. Many stately homes, gardens, and landscapes could be viewed by merely contacting the head gardener or housekeeper and paying them token fees for a "tour." It should also be noted that the provision of open space for sports the design of the public park. This park has become a watershed in recent thinking about the creation and function of public spaces.

The 175-acre former slaughterhouse and cattle-market site is now the largest park in Paris. When the competition for the design was announced, its stated aim was "to realize on the same site the largest Museum of Science, Technology, and Industry and a Music Center." Grand words for an unbuilt public park project still at pre-competition stage, but Parc de la Villette did prove to be a uniquely creative and inventive place.

The La Villette project attracted 471 entries from forty-one countries. The competition was judged by an international jury of twenty-one, with the late Roberto Burle Marx as its chairman. It was won by Bernard Tschumi, architect and chairman of the school of archi-tecture at Columbia University, who describes his design like this:

> La Villette was called a park, but it was not a park;
> it was a new type of city. I have always said it is
> the largest discontinuous city building in Paris.
> Like many of our urban projects today, we were
> starting with an old industrial area, the site of
> slaughterhouses.

The enormous site has been organized on a point grid. At twenty-six points of intersection, there are twenty-six red metal follies. Some of them are abstract metal sculptures; others function as stands where drinks and ice cream are sold. Tschumi also designed

**Below** *The Guadalupe River Park flood-control project was a site-generated design created in the 1990s in San Jose, California.*

two other layers of lines in the form of raised walkways.

Alexandre Chemetoff designed the Bamboo Garden—which lies below the soil grade—and Vexiard, also a French landscape architect, designed the formal Vineyard. Some young designers have been disappointed by their work. However, Lodewijk Baljon, a Dutch landscape architect of about the same age, was more impressed:

> The result is a mannerist plan. It is characterized by unrest, movement, passion, and a tendency toward elegance. It aims to evoke a fantastically ordered chaos with an ingenious mental game; it is admirably suited to a cultural amusement park.

## Duisburg North Landscape Park

The five-hundred-acre site of an abandoned steel factory at Duisburg in the Ruhrgebeit area of central Germany has been transformed. Four years after the factory was closed, it was suggested that the site should be made into a park. An international competition for the design was won by Professor Peter Latz and his colleague, Anna-Liese Latz. In 1994 the park was opened, but work will continue here for many years.

Duisburg North is budgeted at 28 million pounds, and it is part of a 117-square-mile regeneration project in an area that boasted some of the most advanced steel factories in the world. In fact, the buildings and the enormous machinery have been left intact and incorporated into the design.

Initially, an analysis was made of the existing vegetation, all the major structures, and the railroad network that formerly served the factory. Latz saw the railroad, with its complexity and superb engineering, as a form of land art, and he incorporated it into the

**Below** *The Interopolis Garden, Tilburg, the Netherlands. The triangular five-acre site is near Breda, southeast of Rotterdam. A large, tectonic-shaped lily pool is finished with wooden slabs that can be used as seating.*

design. Where the rail structure had broken down, he designed high-level walkways to improve access and to give views over the site.

Many of the existing materials on the site have been recycled to serve new purposes. Aggregate for cement has been made from salvaged bricks, and large metal plates made of pig iron have been blasted clean with compressed air to become giant pavers laid in sand to make a plaza: the Piazza Metallica. The run-off water from sidewalks, roofs, and roads has been channeled into a polluted waste-water canal that has been diverted into former cooling tanks and old settling basins. As a result, the water on the whole site has been purified.

The design concept for the landscape is not entirely unified because the site is so large; it is a design realized in several layers. Latz initially submitted plans for five separate parks that would have been superimposed on one another during installation. On further consideration, he designed seven satellite areas nearer to the workers' housing and away from the main park. Here he located sports stadiums, children's playgrounds, and other areas defined by leisure activities.

Latz has a clear view of the role of Duisberg Park: "This is to become a historical park, but the history starts now and goes forward as well as backward." The park is well used by the local population. Rock bands play in the open air, groups of mountain-climbing enthusiasts scale the taller blast furnaces, and ex–worker families promenade on the overhead walkways.

## Guadalupe River Park

The Guadalupe River, which runs through the city of San Jose, California, can become a destructive and raging torrent when it is at flood tide. The city did

**Below** *The Minneapolis Federal Courthouse Plaza contains sculptural earth mounds based on glacial drumlins and logs. These are symbols of inherited memory. They represent the hills and trees seen by the first settlers in Minnesota.*

**Above** *The former Thyssen steelworks in Ruhr, Duisburg North, has been transformed into a public park. This is the spring garden in the former pig-iron smelting area.*

not want the standard government-agency solution of ugly concrete culverts enclosing the entire three-mile stretch of water in order to protect the town and its citizens when the river was on the rampage. For this reason, Hargreaves & Associates was asked to solve the problem of creating a preventative measure that was also aesthetically pleasing.

George Hargreaves headed a multidisciplinary team that consisted of civil, hydraulic, structural and geotechnical engineers, and environmental consultants, as well as fourteen additional review agencies. Their collective aim in this project was to realize the city's vision for their river and its use.

The design concept for the area consisted of two distinct layers. One, the "underlay" as Hargreaves calls it, was to increase the depth and the width of the river channel so it could accommodate the flood tide when necessary. Two, the "overlay," involved shoring up the banks with runs of gabions (tough wire cubes containing either rocks or soil for planting) to retain the river bank organically and to underpin the path and planting system.

In section, the goal was to read from river to the gabion to a generous path for walking or bicycling to, in parts, graceful stone retaining steps doubling as seats. Trees and shrubs have been planted along the entire section of the river. These plants look very attractive, and they also help to stabilize the earth structure of the bank.

In places the riverbank was totally flat. Here, raised and shaped earth forms were designed, both for their visual impact and so they could act as a reinforcement during flood time. The total cost of the project was $50 million.

## Scan Park

Scan Park was designed by Sven-Ingar Andersson in 1997. The completed park is an example of his

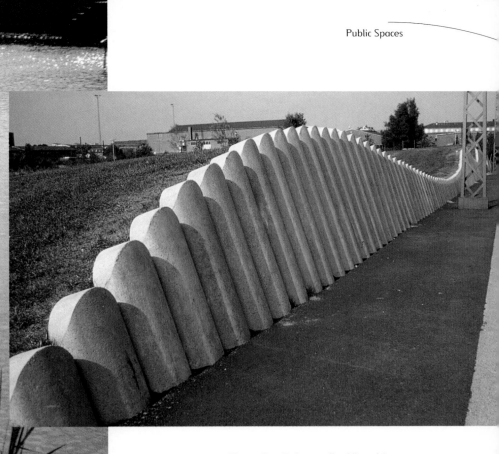

**Above** *Scan Park, a small public park in Copenhagen, Denmark, has beautiful walls retaining undulating grassed landforms.*

**Center** *The serpentine pond walk creates a contrast with the sculptural, rolling-wave landforms in Scan Park.*

most skilled work as a mature designer. It is a small public park situated in a bleak industrial suburb of Copenhagen. The project was initiated when a developer wanted to build a business center that would be used by many companies. As an initial move, the developer wanted to create an attractive park at the entrance to his land. The competition for the park was won by Andersson.

Andersson has played sinuously with the main elements of the design. The largest part of the ground planes is a lawn consisting of six rolling earth forms. Seen in section from the street side of the park, the rolling shapes are retained with a run of close-set pale yellow concrete stone palings. The curved tops of the palings are a striking variation on the rolling forms of the lawn: a sturdy, simple, and beautiful design element.

The lawn-covered forms slope down to meet seamlessly at a large pond with an undulating serpentine edge, which has been created by a generous asphalt path retained by neat rusty steel sections; the serpentine shape is further reinforced by a ribbon beach of pebbles that runs along the pond. It is a serpentine with a difference, recalling the image of Alvar Aalto's rippling modern classic vase design, the Lake.

Gentle troughs next to the path contain groups of tall aquatic plants creating a contrast in height, color, and texture. The tallest vertical contrasts are two twenty-five-foot-high pipes at the shallow end of the pond, one rusty and one stainless steel; water flows out from their tops. Andersson was inspired by the stems of tall bamboo.

On the opposite side of the pond is a six-foot-high wooden fence. It echoes the vertical foliage of the aquatic plants and fountains and masks the near-derelict site beyond. Andersson is pleased to see that the park has become a playground for the children from the public housing project nearby.

# Private Spaces

Residential design is the most intricate, specialized, demanding, and frustrating field for the landscape designer.

Garrett Eckbo

The private garden has not been a focus of attention for landscape architects and designers since about 1980. Their energies have been devoted to the design of public spaces. This trend reflects an economic reality. Only by accepting large-scale commissions can they be assured of a large enough client base to support their offices. In other words, they have had to "follow the money."

Two very distinct strands of design for private spaces have emerged in the latter part of the twentieth century. The first is naturalistic and is characterized by mainly herbaceous planting. The

**Left** *The spines of agave leaves in the foreground were the inspiration for the large, sculptural shapes of the structures in this Arizona garden.*

**Below** *The Barragán-inspired walls in a suburban garden in South San Francisco. The owner of the garden is an Indian expatriate. The walls washed in the vivid colors of the subcontinent personalize his private space.*

other, opposing strand might be called a "smartening up." It is characterized by a sculptural approach, inspired by the intrinsic nature of the site.

The naturalistic approach to design has its roots in the planting style of German parks and is now also popular in Holland and the United States. At the end of the 1980s, this trend in civic design triggered a formulaic, ecological, and naturalistic style of planting in contemporary private gardens. At their best, the results are simplistic. At their worst, they represent a "dumbing down" of landscape and garden design.

The opposing, more sculptural style of design is practiced by some designers in the United States and Europe who are not concerned solely with plants per se. By using various contemporary materials, they make gardens that reflect certain aspects of contemporary culture and have something to say about this particular moment in history.

These two approaches to garden design are very distinct. However, they both reflect the fact that the private garden has had to adapt to social and economic pressure. Generally, private gardens are very much smaller than their counterparts in the nineteenth and early twentieth centuries. This is due largely to the enormous social changes wrought since World War II, such as the high cost of maintenance and labor. Groundcover plants have become more popular because they reduce maintenance costs to a minimum. The suburban lawn has begun to be modified as more and more young couples create simple, tough gardens that suit the needs of their growing children as well as the family pets. Environmental change has also left its mark as dry or even drought conditions predicate a corresponding plant palette. Finally, a renewed interest in naturalistic, ecological plantings has reduced the popularity of exotics. This has led a great number of garden centers to narrow the choice of plants they offer.

The naturalistic, ecological style was thoroughly investigated in a series of lectures given in London in

**Below** *In this private Arizona garden an iridescent serpentine wall clothed with green glass mosaic encloses a terrace used for entertaining.*

**Right** *A bold and simple design for a private garden in Holland. The paths and fences are attractively made, and there are stepping stones in the pond.*

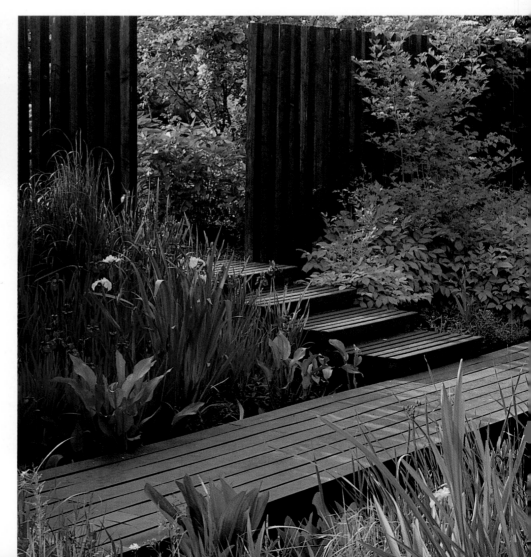

March 1999. The event was an opportunity to hear the views of landscape architects and designers such as Piet Oudolf of Holland, Dan Pearson of Great Britain, and James van Sweden of the United States, all of them practitioners of a mainly naturalistic style.

By the end of the day, we both yearned for some structure that went beyond the hard landscaping of just a few roads, paths, and the occasional summerhouse (admittedly of a highly contemporary design). Our senses were clamoring for any structure beyond that provided by perennial herbaceous plantings.

Oudolf, Pearson, and van Sweden all spoke at length about the sculptural beauty of dried stems and seedheads in the fall and winter. We felt great sympathy for Mary Keen, the British garden writer and designer, whose view of naturalistic planting is rather similar to our own. As she put it, a garden that is "basically brown" (said in her unique, orotund, and ironic tone) for four or five months of the year is not terribly attractive. Keen also criticized the intrinsically limited palette of naturalistic, herbaceous planting. Like us, she felt that the endless drifts of

sedums, rudbeckias, salvias, and polygonums were not really diverse or interesting enough to fully engage the eye and brain.

This book offers several examples of gardens that stand in opposition to the naturalistic approach. Many of them could be characterized by Robert Irwin's definition of site-generated design. One such example is a private garden in London that was designed to take account of the intrinsic nature of the site, the history of the house, and, most important of all, the personal interests of the client.

The design evolved in the following way. The designers were invited to meet the clients and to see what they described as "a very small garden patch at the back of the house and a few broken-down plant containers at the front." The initial discussion was stereotypical, covering all of the usual questions relevant to a small London garden. The breakthrough occurred when the designers were invited up to the living room. Here they saw that their client was a collector of works by young British artists. The bookcase was filled with books about land art and

**Above** *Sky reflected in the dark gray interior of a swimming pool in a private garden in Madrid. The clipped mounds of escallonia are reminiscent of the organic shapes of azaleas in Japanese gardens.*

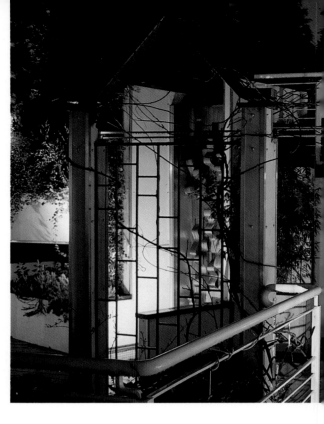

modern artists such as David Hockney, Gordon Matta-Clark, Frank Stella, and Andy Warhol. At this point, the idea of a nice, conventional solution to the design of the backyard was abandoned in favor of something that would reflect the clients' own interests. Given this opportunity, the clients declared that they would really like to see stone, metal, and moss used in a low-maintenance garden.

Over the next three months, the design gradually evolved. It encompassed a pink, Indian-stone terrace adjacent to the house. Moss was planted along the fractured edge of one side of the terrace. A smooth concrete three-foot-high diagonal was built from the house, across the terrace, and then into the lawn at its grade level. This structure, which provides seating on the terrace, is edged along its entire length with a narrow stripe of blue mosaic in Hockney's Los Angeles swimming-pool blue. Steps on one side of the terrace lead to the upper level of the garden. Here, the ground plane is surfaced with bitumen-set gravel.

Three rusting, cast-iron, eighteenth-century European-style urns from China were arranged on the concrete seating structure. These were a reference to the house, which is also eighteenth century, and they could be used as planters for seasonal flowers. A circular pavilion measuring eleven feet in diameter was also installed. It is built of the steel mesh used for reinforcing concrete and has a blue circular cover made of tensile material that can be roped on in summer.

The wittiest element of all is an arc of lawn that runs along one side of the circular pavilion. This amused the client since it was a reference to the arc work of Gordon Matta-Clark. The client also understood that it doubled as a reference to the English lawn. Even though it was only ten feet long and four inches wide, he wondered if he would be able to maintain it to an "adequate standard."

Sites like this small London garden and the naturalistic style represent two main strands of landscape architecture and design. Viewed this way, they give some idea of the diversity of work being done in the latter part of the twentieth century.

**Center top** *Images projected onto both sides of a video screen play continuously in a suburban garden in north London. The garden's owner is amused by images of historic gardens such as Hampton Court, Hestercombe, and Versailles.*

**Center bottom** *An international businessman uses this Johannesburg garden for meditation. The carp pond bounded by rocks is evocative of the serene courtyard gardens of Japan.*

**Far right** *A Tokyo courtyard garden created by a leading Japanese artist, potter, and film maker. The brilliant effect of his "river of moss" proves that gardens can be made by non–landscape artists.*

**Right** *These fish stepping stones are on the Sea Terrace of the Jonathan Parker Abramson Safe Harbor Roof Garden at the Beth Israel North Hospital in New York. Recuperating children use the rubber stepping stones as an aid to retrieving a sense of balance after long illnesses.*

# Healing Gardens

**Left** *Convalescing children regaining motor control at water and sand tables. The rubber tubes in the background are part of a thirty-foot-long rubber sound sculpture connected to the Octopus Table. The sculpture is activated by children talking into the tubing.*

A landscape for people with life-threatening illnesses is going to be a different kind of place from your typical open park. It should have enclosed, connected rooms that provide a safe haven. A family huddled together sobbing, you don't want to share. And there should be lots of botanical complexity, but it should be ordered, not sloppy. Disease represents disorder, and that's the last thing a patient needs.

Topher Delaney

Delaney is a leading American landscape architect and artist who designed her first healing garden near San Francisco while recovering from cancer. More recently, she has designed healing gardens for the San Diego Children's Hospital and New York's Beth Israel Hospital, a garden south of San Francisco for Alzheimer's patients, and a meditation garden at the Norris Cancer Center in Los Angeles funded by a family whose daughter had died at the center. Healing gardens create a sense of community, and in no other area of

**Left** *This twenty-foot-high metal fence encloses the terrace of the Safe Harbor Roof Garden. It was made by Sarah Keizer, who encloses children's fantasies within cartoon silhouettes of twenty of Manhattan's bridges.*

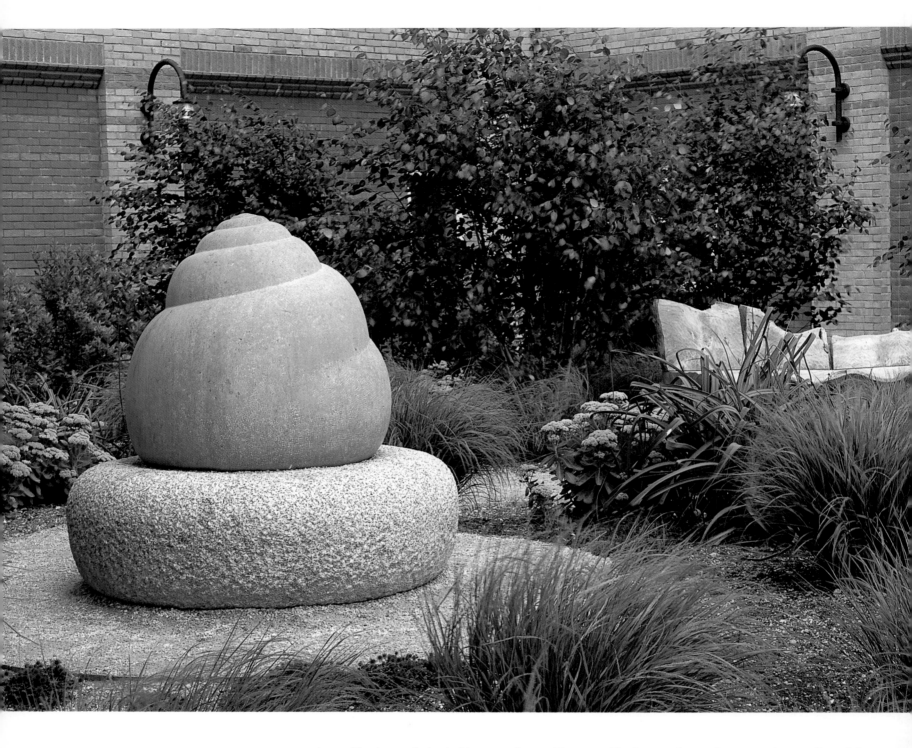

garden and landscape design is this more relevant. The gardens designed by Delaney have often been funded by donations and built with volunteer labor.

The idea of the garden as a place of healing has its roots in ancient history. In Egypt, gardens were designed specially for patients with mental illnesses. Gardens of healing, solitude, and sanctuary were also part of life in the great monasteries and abbeys of medieval Europe. Monte Cassino in Italy, Cluny in France, Monserrat in Spain, and Fountains Abbey in England were some of the most historically important.

Healing gardens reflect an understanding of the human need to be in contact with nature and the natural processes of growth and renewal. The instinct to create gardens of this kind has emerged once again in the late twentieth century. This is the century that has brought us keyhole surgery, chemotherapy, and laser technology, but despite huge medical advances, the high-rise hospitals of our time cannot provide all of the curative answers. Environmental and behavioral psychologists have been working to prove the benefits of bringing gardens and landscapes to patients.

Research at Harvard University has shown that the response of patients is improved by contact with a natural environment.

In the United States there are over 150 hospitals and day centers that have gardens or greenhouses devoted to horticultural therapy programs. By creating therapeutic gardens, they are also taking a lead in humanizing the "hard settings" of most hospitals and hospices. A therapeutic garden often has to meet the needs of two different categories of patient. There are those needing short-term rehabilitation and those with long-term degenerative diseases.

Dr. Roger Ulrich, an environmental psychologist at Texas A & M College of Architecture, has undertaken a ten-year research project focusing on the relationship between patient well-being and the environment. He has found that patients whose rooms overlook brick walls need more painkillers and longer recuperation time than patients who have views of a natural landscape from their beds. Similar studies show that maximum sunlight and contact with the natural world reduce patient anxiety levels.

Several gardens have been designed on the fifty-two-acre campus of the new eighty-bed acute-care department of the St. Michael Health Care Center in Texarkana, Arkansas. The gardens are the result of an environmental psychologist and a landscape architect working together to provide a more humane setting for the hospital's patients.

James Burnett, the landscape designer on the project, had seen his mother die in a small room overlooking a gravel roof. Talking about the experience, he said: "I would like to have gotten her out of there. She lived on a lake, and she just wanted to go home." He was left with the conviction that his practice should change direction and devote itself to the design of gardens and landscapes for hospitals.

The architect W. Kirk Hamilton worked with Burnett. Their aim was to create buildings and gardens that would provide compassionate settings for healing as well as dignified places in which to die. In describing his motivation, Burnett says: "It's tragic that people today have to leave the planet in these unbearable situations. They're like prisons: tiny little rooms with people coming in and jabbing you, and TVs blaring all down the hall."

On the St. Michael site, Burnett preserved as many existing trees as possible and planted more in the gently rolling woodland divided by two streams. His master plan included nine fountains, a lake fed by wells that became the reservoir for irrigation, and a series of jogging paths through the woods. The circulation paths are logical and well marked. In the large courtyards of the hospital, a simple bicolor paving pattern was used, and one of the fountains offers access for wheelchair users. Seasonal plantings include azalea, crape myrtle, pear trees, and spiraea.

In the early 1990s, David Kamp, a landscape designer who used to plan estates in Connecticut, decided that he would devote his professional time and skills to designing gardens for AIDS patients. His first project, the Schnaper Memorial Garden, was a terrace adjacent to the AIDS section at Cardinal Cook Hospital in New York City. The powerful medications the patients take make their eyes very sensitive to bright sunlight. To counter the overbright, sunny aspect of the terrace, Kamp designed shaded seating. He also provided low planters that would allow wheelchair-bound patients to garden actively. They grew herbs, vegetables, and flowers that were picked and used to brighten up the patients' rooms.

Kamp worked with the Tamarind Foundation, a not-for-profit organization in New York. He and Bruce Detrick, another founding member, worked to achieve the group's goal of helping to provide an

**Left** *An Art in Hospitals project in Worthing, England. This piece is called* Shell, *and it was made by Peter Randall-Page in 1997. The sculptural bench is by Steve Geliot. It creates a contrast with the restrained plantings of* Sedum spectabile *'Autumn Joy' and the grass* Stipa arundinacea, *which lends gentle sound and movement to this healing garden.*

improved life for AIDS sufferers. As with so many other healing gardens in existence, this project was funded by private donations.

Sedgemoor Commons, Falmouth, Maine, has a garden designed for Alzheimer's patients by Robert Hoover, a local landscape architect. His design for the five-acre site is based on what he calls "remembrance therapy." He views the disease as "life in fast-forward reverse." He has identified three stages of the disease, which he sees as a reversal of the normal aging process. At the onset of the disease, Alzheimer's patients are adults. The "reversal" to which Hoover refers means that they end their lives as infants.

Sedgemoor Commons is built in the shape of a clover leaf. Each wing is named after a major American poet: the Hawthorne wing is for residential care,

*Far right  The courtyard healing garden was created from a sterile space in the Marin Cancer Center, north of San Francisco.*

*Above  The Norris Cancer Center, Los Angeles, is a large meditation garden. The walls reflect the influence of Luis Barragán.*

Longfellow is for nursing care, and the Millay is for advanced nursing care. This continuum of care is unique in the treatment of Alzheimer's. Hoover has made a garden for each wing of the hospital. The gardens are designed to help patients at each stage of the disease. All of them have extremely secure fencing and generous, easily identifiable paths.

The Hawthorne garden is used by patients with the early stages of Alzheimer's. Honeysuckles, roses, and lilacs are planted here, to help patients focus on earlier times in their lives. A clothesline, basketball hoop, and

gazebo are intended to give the patients some sense of autonomy, exploration, and control. Another of Hoover's main objectives with these gardens is to "bring back choice into the lives" of people institutionalized and suffering from an irreversible disease.

The Longfellow garden is centered on the second stage of Alzheimer's, which is the emotional equivalent of adolescence. The arbor provides a sense of enclosure and safety. Eight hawthorn trees are spaced in pairs on grassed plots around the garden's main quadrangle. The plantings emphasize tones of green rather than flowers. The planting includes arborvitae, viburnum, spiraea, periwinkle, and magnolia.

The much smaller and more intimate Millay garden is for the third stage of the disease and beyond. Hoover emphasized security and serenity in this Japanese-inspired space. Here there is a dry stream bed with glacial river stone and specimen weathered fieldstone within plantings of Siberian iris, snow-in-summer, and kousa dogwood. Lilac, roses, and honeysuckles on either side of a path reinforce the sense of safety and security. The adjacent beds are planted with Himalayan birch, hay-scented fern, witch hazel, and bayberry.

Patients with long-term mental impairment or psychological problems also benefit from contact with plants and gardening. Dr. Oliver Sacks, a neurologist and author of *Awakenings* and *The Man Who Mistook His Wife for a Hat*, refers to the stress-reducing qualities of plants on his patients: "I had people who were so anxious in the hospital that I would do my consultations in the greenhouse. They would often feel less pressured there and have less ticks and involuntary movements." He has watched patients in deep dementia—"who could not tell a knife from a fork"— begin to plant: "They do not put a plant upside down, and no matter how estranged the mental state, they have a deep sense of how plants grow."

In England, the West Dorset Hospital in Dorchester and the Royal Brompton Heart and Lung Hospital in London both have courtyard gardens for their patients. At St. Thomas Hospital in London, the River Thames–side garden next to the hospital doubles as a public park and a garden for the patients.

A New Design Aesthetic

# Place

**Previous pages** *Trump Towers, New York City. More property developers should consider planting trees on the facades of their unimaginative steel-and-glass skyscrapers.*

In the landscape, the context is everything, from the cosmos to the park, so the real question is, What idea arises out of that?

George Hargreaves

Post-industrial sites, the plazas of new towns, office buildings, shopping centers, corporate headquarters, river and harbor sites, healing gardens, memorial and sculpture parks: it is in these contexts that contemporary landscape and garden designers work. They focus on improving the site, making it more useful, more expressive, and capable of giving greater pleasure to the public.

In the past, landscape architects and designers were employed almost exclusively by clients wanting grand private or quasi-private gardens. Today, the situation has changed entirely. While the designers of the past invested heavily in creating a sense of place in a limited number of private gardens, today's designers are concerned chiefly with the transformation of a huge and diverse range of places.

Robert Irwin, an abstract painter turned landscape designer, was commissioned to design the Lower Central Garden for the Getty Center, Los Angeles. Irwin's designs are always site generated—that is, inspired by the natural features of the landscape in which it is to be created. It develops from the existing site rather than being imposed upon it.

Since the 1980s Irwin has become internationally famous for his site-generated works in public spaces. In these works he often makes use of topographical features and natural plantings. He made the following statement in relation to the thought processes involved in the development of his design for the Getty garden in Los Angeles:

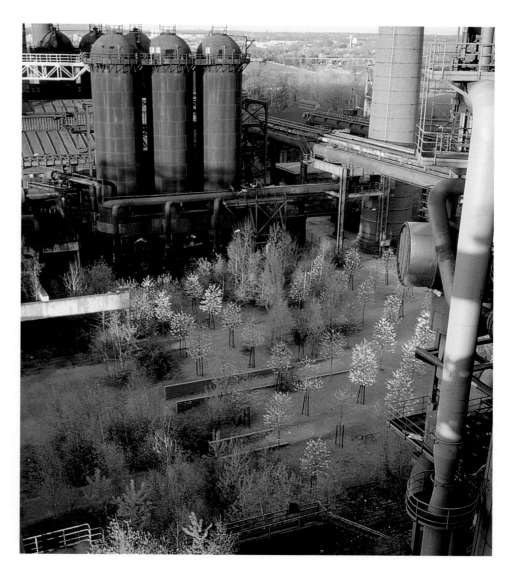

I began with a set of circumstances. As such, every decision had to make sense within the context of a set of cues. In this case, of course, the surrounding architecture was key. This was not going to be a garden off in a field some place. I accepted its architectural setting—which was all but overpowering—but that, in turn, raised other questions. For how do you go from such a surround —from buildings like that—down to a flower? So

**Above** *This former steel factory in Germany has been transformed into a public park. Trees have had a humanizing influence on the site. The blast furnaces are lit on weekends.*

**Far left** *A series of pools on the edge of Lake Lucerne, Switzerland, with the "borrowed landscape" of the mountains.*

you can see this petal, that stalk? I began to think in terms of starting from geometry, compounding the geometry to pattern and the pattern to texture. And in doing so in both directions—from the flower out to the buildings, and from the buildings back to the flower.

Irwin is not alone in creating site-generated landscapes. As George Hargreaves says "The context is everything." This is another way of defining the basis for site-generated design. An article written by Melinda Wortz in *Artforum* in 1981 provides a detailed analysis of Irwin's philosophy of design:

> The content of Irwin's art derives from the presence of the site where the artist works. Presence for Irwin is so much more than just visual phenomena—it is the impression the site presents to all of the senses of the body and the mind. The physical structure expressed in a response to this presence acts as metaphor for the location it occupies. The art's content is both autonomous in its presence [and] wholly integrated with its context. In the end, the work assumes a symbolic power, in the true meaning of the word "symbol." Unlike the traditional symbols, Irwin's work does not refer to the presence of some other thing, but to what is immediately here.

One of Irwin's earliest site-generated works was created at Wellesley College, outside Boston, Massachusetts, in 1979. During an initial visit to the college, Irwin was "struck by the grace of the nature on the campus. How beautiful it all was, and without any intrusion by me." He created *Filigreed Line*, a line or low wall of brushed stainless steel 120 feet long that sliced through the landscape of venerable trees and gently rolling lawns. It spans a low hollow between some beautiful trees, fronting a pond in the middle distance. Abstracted leaf and branch patterns were cut out randomly along its length using a highly sophisticated plasma metal-cutting technique. At its two ends, the metal wall is only a few inches above the ground. In the middle it rises to three feet, where it is supported by concrete footings. When the shadows

*Below* The asymmetrical design of this contemporary rooftop garden makes a striking contrast with the spectacular view of the ultra-conservative City of London below.

from the leaves and branches from the nearby trees play on the metal cut-out images, it is a subtle and beautiful fusion of art and nature—an effect aimed at by many landscape designers. Some time after the installation, Irwin wrote:

> The Wellesley site was so lovely and pastoral, it really didn't require anything additional from me. All I was trying to do with my gesture, in the most subliminal fashion I could manage, and thanks to the reflectivity of the steel and the shimmer of the pond beyond it (the screen often just seemed to disappear)—was to, in a sense, underline the beauty and perceptual vitality of the site as it already existed.

The subtlety of much of Irwin's work in the landscape may not capture the immediate imaginations of many onlookers, but his influence on gardens and landscapes and on the sense of place in the late twentieth century is of great importance and has far-reaching consequences. It is all about seeing the context.

*Left  A site-generated sculpture in a eucalyptus grove at the University of California, San Diego. The blue chain-link fence takes its color from the bluish cast of the leaves.*

*Below  A garden makeover design, including a swimming pool, on a Phoenix, Arizona, hillside, overlooking Paradise Valley suburb. Indigenous planting around the pool reinforces the sense of place.*

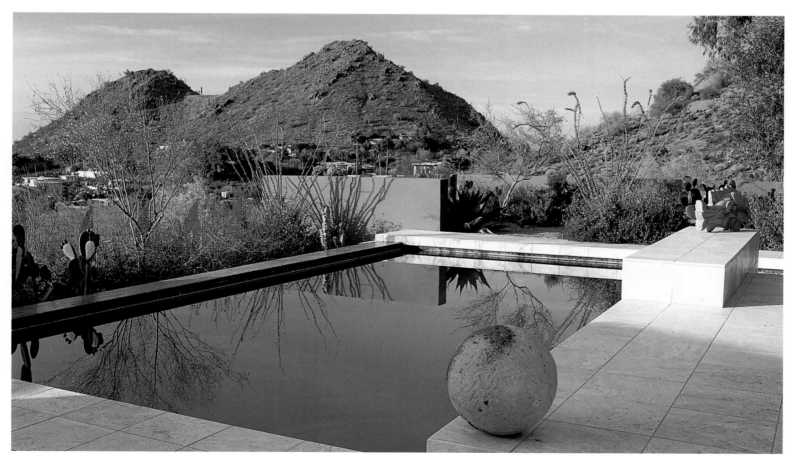

# Space, Scale, and Form

Designs shall be three dimensional.
People live in volumes, not planes.

Garrett Eckbo

**Above** *Contemporary focusing of space, scale, and form in a small private garden in London.*

Space and scale create and reinforce each other. In the contemporary garden and landscape, we find a great diversity of designs. There are those that use perspective and the orthogonal, and others based on the diagonal, the sculptural, or the ecological. In the midst of this diversity, the force of the formal and geometric can still be felt.

The great formal gardens of sixteenth-century Italy and seventeenth-century France were four-square, perpendicular ground extensions of the "footprint" of the villas and palaces that they embellished. When perspective was rediscovered in Renaissance Italy by Brunelleschi and Alberti, great architects patronized by the Medici, it became a prime tool for establishing the center line or axial spine of a garden. This was often a wide central path, as at the Boboli Gardens in Florence or at Versailles, from which all the other elements were scaled. Transverse paths, square or rectilinear flowerbeds, allées of trees, urns, basins, and water jets were all common features.

Garden designers such as Michelozzo in Italy and Le Nôtre in France adopted many painterly tricks. A flat plane could be made to seem three-dimensional through the use of one, two, or three lines leading back to a vanishing point. Converging parallels created an illusion of space on a two-dimensional ground plane, a trick that exaggerated the depth of the site. Finally, geometric shapes were used to foreshorten both the garden space and the objects within it. Orthogonal space and scale were most widely used during the nineteenth century in Europe and the United States, where the style was defined as the Beaux-Arts.

In the twentieth century, the use of orthogonal, formal principles of space and form has been reinterpreted by designers such as Daniel Urban Kiley in the United States and Fernando Caruncho in Spain. Examples of their work are shown in the case study section.

The diagonal use of garden space is unique to the twentieth century. This new approach, which is rooted

**Above** *There is an interplay between the different forms of the undulating lawns and the immaculate walls in this large garden surrounding a multinational corporation's headquarters near Paris.*

in the 1930s, is in direct opposition to the orthogonal layout. The Beaux-Arts style of the nineteenth century eventually gave way to a new form of twentieth-century landscape architecture. This new style drew on the influences of Cubism, Art Deco, the International Style of modern architecture spearheaded by Le Corbusier, and the work of the Bauhaus personified by Walter Gropius.

Gropius became the head of architecture at Harvard University in 1938. There were three students in the landscape-architecture department who were especially inspired by his lectures: Daniel Urban Kiley, James C. Rose, and Garrett Eckbo. Rose and Eckbo

freeing the landscape from the axial designs of traditional, Beaux-Arts formality and the rediscovery of the diagonal, the zigzag, and the sculptural.

These new modes of dealing with space and scale were inspired by Picasso, Theo van Doesberg, Mies van der Rohe, Wassily Kandinsky, and Naum Gabo. The influence of their work led Eckbo to make use of the abstract in his designs. He was also profoundly influenced by Gabriel Guevrekian and Pierre-Emile Legrain, Cubist or Art Deco designers from Paris in the 1920s. It was a design by Legrain that gave Eckbo his life-long obsession with zigzag paths for establishing space and scale, especially in small urban gardens.

**Below** *Swirling drifts of ground-plane planting contrast with the verticals of pampas grass in this garden in Brazil.*

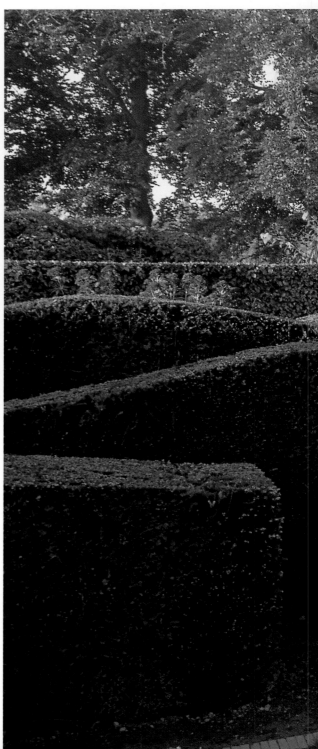

**Right** *Sculpted yew hedges enclose the spaces of this naturalistic garden made by a Dutch designer.*

were to have a major influence on the profession in the years after World War II. Two other influential figures from the pre– and post–World War II period were Thomas Church in California and Christopher Tunnard in Great Britain.

Eckbo is an iconoclastic and truly revolutionary landscape designer. Seen as a representative of the modern in landscape architecture both in the United States and abroad, he is credited with two primary innovations:

Eckbo wrote an article defining his concept of space and scale in landscape architecture and its relationship to sculpture:

Architecture (like sculpture) . . . works with three-dimensional volumes, but their arrangement is governed by the human activities they must shelter . . . Yet sculpture is also analogous to landscape design, for the handling of ground masses can be carried out with a truly sculptural set of forms in relation. In fact, landscape architecture may be considered more analogous to sculpture, since its forms are moulded and carved and grouped, whereas those in architecture are constructed.

Although Eckbo designed gardens for private clients in Bel Air, his true obsession was with integrating aesthetic and social values. Many of his most visionary projects involved public housing for migrant workers at the end of the Great Depression. He described his work as "the arrangement of environments for people." He may have been inspired by Bauhaus theories regarding the social responsibility of all the arts.

As a student, Eckbo published a paper entitled "Small Gardens in the City," which contained eighteen different layouts for a standard, rectangular, fenced urban garden. The layouts show an oblique skewing of the plans, terraces, walkways, plantings, abstract

**Above** *A geometric planting of thistles in a meadow at the garden festival at the Château de Chaumont in France demonstrates a witty use of space.*

arcs, and, in each case, some use of the diagonal. Eckbo drew his inspiration from the art of the early part of the twentieth century. This may account for the continued relevance of his designs, since this period in the history of art continues to hold sway today.

In 1993, Eckbo gave a reworked commentary on his 1937 small gardens model:

■ Gardens are places in which people live out of doors.

■ Gardens must be the homes of delight, of gaiety, of fantasy, of illusion, of imagination, of adventure.

■ Designs shall be areal, not axial.

■ Design shall be dynamic, not static.

We were fortunate to meet Eckbo briefly in December 1997. We took the opportunity to ask him what he thought was Gropius's single most important influence all those years ago at Harvard. Eckbo replied most succinctly: "Art was the ground-breaker."

Ecological awareness, which began to emerge in the late 1960s and early 1970s, became a primary influence on the design of gardens and landscapes in the late twentieth century. In an ecological project, the scale is determined by the indigenous plants and trees on the proposed site. The ability to respond to the ecology of a site has become a part of every landscape architect's and designer's battery of basic professional skills.

**Above** *An allée of fastigiate oaks screens the offices of the Banque de Luxembourg from the boundary line of an adjacent property.*

Ian McHarg leads the field on the subject of ecology in landscape design. He has been teaching landscape architecture at the University of Pennsylvania since 1954. His course, entitled "Human Ecological Planning," has provided a basis for the ecological-planning movement worldwide. McHarg published *Design with Nature* in 1972, which has become an ecological manifesto for the planning and design profession and for urban ecologists. The book was an attack on the uncontrolled building and desecration of natural habitats that occurred after World War II.

Inevitably, it was felt that some university landscape departments and professional landscape architecture practices overemphasized McHarg's vision. It was said that the aesthetic—a vital aspect of

**Below** *A contemporary minimalist, serial form of spatial design is used to organize a traditional "potager" in the courtyard of a ferme omée in northern France.*

landscape architecture and design—had become subservient to planning and ecology. McHarg responded to this criticism:

> I can't believe that design can proceed without knowledge of the natural environment and the social environment . . . [Design and planning] are complementary . . . I don't think [they are] adversarial at all.

Our personal view is that if the importance of ecological considerations in determining the space and scale of a landscape is overemphasized, the ultimate result is a denial of history and culture, with all the riches that they can bring.

The concepts of space and scale in contemporary gardens and landscapes have been fundamentally influenced by three men: Luis Barragán, Roberto

Burle Marx, and Isamu Noguchi, who have the status of icons within the landscape profession.

Barragán originally trained as an engineer. The minimalist, rectilinear aesthetic of his work has inspired three generations of architects and landscape designers. Islamic influences from Spain and Morocco can be seen in the space and scale of his projects. This merged neatly with his interest in the buildings of Le Corbusier and the International Style. Planar walls, often washed in the bright colors of his native Mexico, planes of water in square or rectilinear pools, and more water falling from channels at the ends of linear walls are all features of his designs.

Burle Marx studied painting in Berlin during the 1920s. A visit to the botanic garden in Berlin led him to discover the beauty of plants from his native

**Above** *This Mexican-influenced design in El Paso, Texas, demonstrates a sculptural use of form and scale.*

country, Brazil. The paintings of Joan Miró and the biomorphic sculptures of Jean Arp inspired him to design drifts of rounded, free-flowing planting on a huge scale. The scale of his garden and landscape designs attracted modern architects. His designs were perceived both as an adjunct and a contrast to the buildings they enclosed. Oscar Niemeyer commissioned him to design the landscape for Brasilia. Burle Marx's other masterpiece is in Rio de Janeiro. It is the

three-mile-long Copacabana promenade with its bold, serpentine, bicolor pattern: a hard landscaping variation on the drifts and swirls of planting in his gardens and landscapes.

Noguchi was a Japanese-American sculptor. As a student in Paris, he worked with Constantin Brancusi. Space and scale in Noguchi's work in the landscape were an amalgam of both Western ideas and an Eastern aesthetic. Modern materials such

**Right** *In a park adjacent to a main train station in Barcelona, seating takes the form of a large, multilevel spiral edged in ceramic tiles and defined by trees that provide shade. The 1992 Olympic Games were the impetus for a series of public parks created across the city by architects, civil engineers, and artists.*

as steel and marble fountains were juxtaposed and contrasted with large natural stones.

Noguchi's last great work is called *California Scenario*. It is located in the plaza of some office buildings at Costa Mesa, California, south of Los Angeles. The design was inspired by the image of early settlers trudging across the Sierra Nevada and Cascade Mountains to the Golden State. Noguchi has abstracted from that experience and yet conveyed its reality: a serpentine water course dives down the angle of a sluice shape used for processing gold; an angled grass and flower meadow is bounded by redwood trees; and a sandy, gravel hillock is planted with cacti. Two stainless-steel fountains here are an allusion to twentieth-century mechanization. The use of space and scale in this layout continues to inspire landscape architects and designers today.

# Color and Texture

A good garden must be a piece of art. The basic principles of contrast, texture, dimension, and proportion [are] very important to understand. But there must be an idea!

Roberto Burle Marx

Color and texture of amazing diversity have emerged in garden and landscape design since 1980, the moment at which garden designers and landscape architects began to use a brighter and more varied palette in their designs. This new range of color can be seen in both the natural and the artificial materials shown in this book. Many of them are the "signatures" of the work by designers in the case study section.

The tendency to use a brighter and more exciting selection of colors is the result of a diverse collection of influences over the course of the twentieth century. At the end of the nineteenth century and the beginning of the twentieth, there were the wonderfully mad mosaics by Antonio Gaudí in Barcelona and a few of the major Art Nouveau icons such as Charles Rennie Mackintosh and Joseph Hoffmann, who are still an influence in architecture and the contemporary landscape today. Art Nouveau brought a wide and divergent variety of colors and textures to all of the arts. That movement also paved the way for the many forms of abstraction that were to emerge during the twentieth century and continue to be a source of inspiration today.

New, colorful twentieth-century landscapes also reflect the influence of the works of painters such as Joan Miró, new realist sculptors such as Niki de Saint-Phalle, Jean Tinguely, Yves Klein, and Christo, and works of Pop Art and its Dada precedent in the 1950s

**Above** *These words were cut out of a field of grain using a template projected at night from a negative transparency. It was part of a crop art project undertaken by Pierre Vivant at Warwick University, England, in 1993.*

**Left** *"If a plant is dead, then paint it!": this was the concept of a landscape artist and former stage designer who remade a Virginia garden of dead shrubs by grabbing cans of enamel spraypaint and letting rip.*

**Above** *Gene splicing meets Ryoan-ji meets Boboli: a tiny courtyard becomes an amusing sculptured box of color and texture when viewed from the lunchroom of a microbiology research center. The principal elements are fake boxwood, green gravel, paint, and astroturf.*

and 1960s, represented by Andy Warhol, Jasper Johns, Roy Lichtenstein, Claes Oldenburg, and Robert Indiana in the United States and Richard Hamilton and Eduardo Paolozzi in Great Britain.

One of the leading landscape architects whose work has been much affected by Pop Art is the American Martha Schwartz. Witty, artful, and iconoclastic but above all colorful, Schwartz has, over the past twenty years, outraged, enlightened, and amused her public. She has also caused fury among conventional landscape architects. Having attended the International Federation of Landscape Architects Congress in Florence in the mid-1990s, where most of the speakers should have been either statisticians or accountants, we are not surprised by this reaction.

Schwartz's use of colorful materials ranges from the purple aquarium gravel on the ground plane of her notorious Bagel Garden, built in Boston in 1979, to the astroturfed biological shapes in the Splice Garden created in Cambridge, Massachusetts, in 1986. In 1988, she designed the Rio Shopping Center in Atlanta, where the central incident was serried ranks of plaster frogs painted gold and pointing regimentally toward the main water feature. The 1997 Nexus Kashi 3 Development parking lot is defined by ranks of giant orange disks (we think of rising suns brought back to their native land). In 1996, Schwartz designed the garden of the Davis House in El Paso, Texas. The space is divided into a series of compartments with walls washed in pink, blue, purple, and dark yellow, the colors of the American Southwest.

The use of the sumptuous bougainvillea colors of Mexico washed onto pure planar, rectangular, or square walls is characteristic of the architecture of Luis Barragán, the great Mexican architect. His use of color has been a primary influence on gardens and landscape in the latter part of the twentieth century. Among the many designers influenced by Barragan are two with practices in northern California: Topher Delaney in San Francisco and Peter Walker in Berkeley.

Kathryn Gustafson is a designer who shows great sensitivity to texture in the landscape. This may in part be due to her background in fashion design, where both color and texture are of paramount importance. She maintains that the move from fashion to landscape was nothing more than a change in medium. Instead of making sketches of her designs, she encapsulates her initial concept in clay as a bas-relief. Some of her earlier influences were twentieth-century artists such as the painter Richard Tuttle and the sculptor Dennis Oppenheim.

Hard elements, such as stone, brick, plaster, and metal, all bring texture to the twentieth-century landscape. There is an enormous variety of texture to

be seen in the case study section of this book. Stone is used in numerous different ways: Daniel Urban Kiley's stone retaining walls in Connecticut, layered stone grid patterns by Arata Isozaki in Japan, and the solid stone block seats of Thomas Balsley in Long Island City. There are also satellite-dish sculptures used by Mark Rios in Long Beach, the bougainvillea-colored plaster walls of Topher Delaney in California, rusting steel retaining walls designed by Robert Irwin in Los

**Above** *Images of the terraced rice paddies of the Far East realized in 1997 by students from the Ecole Mediterranée des Jardins et du Paysage de Grasse, France. Woven chestnut wattles sculpt the land and retain the rice plantings.*

**Right** *Glass gravel has been used to create the impression of cones of harvested rice and salt, evoking memories of the designer's home in Vietnam. The gravel's appearance changes constantly in sunshine and moonlight. The garden has been built on a Los Angeles hillside and planted with agaves, lemon grass, and orchids.*

Angeles, aluminum sculpture and screening by Ted Smyth in New Zealand, and cones of sand made by the D.A.ST. artists in Egypt.

Soft landscaping elements can also bring color and texture to a design. The case studies include Fernando Caruncho's Wheat Parterre in Spain, Jacques Wirtz's undulating yew hedges in Paris, the grasses and herbaceous plantings of Ton ter Linden in Holland, the tropical plants of Raymond Jungles in Florida, Jack Lenor Larsen's dune garden in Long Island, a grid of fruit trees designed by Desvigne & Dalnoky in France, Walter Beck's and Lester Collins's mosses at Innisfree in New York State, and the grassed landforms of Kathryn Gustafson, George Hargreaves, and Charles Jencks.

**Above** *Plantings of delicate waving grass and dense stolid succulents: an excellent example of naturalistic planting in large drifts.*

Jacques Wirtz excels at designing gardens with interesting color and texture all year round. One of his largest Belgian gardens is Le Petite Garenne near Antwerp. Beech hedges and raised triangular beds, solid with pennisetum and molinia grasses, are randomly planted and widely spaced cornus and roses, creating an interplay and variation of texture. In spring, the grasses contrast lightly with the verticals of the cornus. The summer green of the grass sets off the red roses. In fall and winter, the pale beige grasses are a stunning counterpoint to the red-gold of the beech hedges that form the basic structure of the garden.

# Rhythm and Movement

Flux and reflux—the rhythm of
change—alternate and persist in
everything under the sky.

Thomas Hardy

"Rhythm is the most important single attribute in landscape design. It is the quality that gives life and joy, motion and repose. It is poetry and song." So said Will Curtis, an American landscape designer and creator of the Garden in the Woods, near Boston. Whether or not one agrees totally with this, he has captured aspects of that elusive quality in his design in a most attractive way.

Rhythm and movement in the contemporary garden derive from the relationships between earth forms, planting, and water incidents, all of which give unity and direction to a design and create an expressive variety of experience. Paths and the movement that they allow, the framing or screening of views, the position of focal and viewing points, changes of level, and the movement of elements such as water and

**Right**  *The ground-plane rhythm is established by serpentine bands of contrasting indigenous grass and wildflowers, enhancing this contemporary landscape in the Napa Valley.*

**Far right**  *Strong, meandering benches make a rhythmic counterpoint to other hard landscaping elements in a public park in Auckland, New Zealand.*

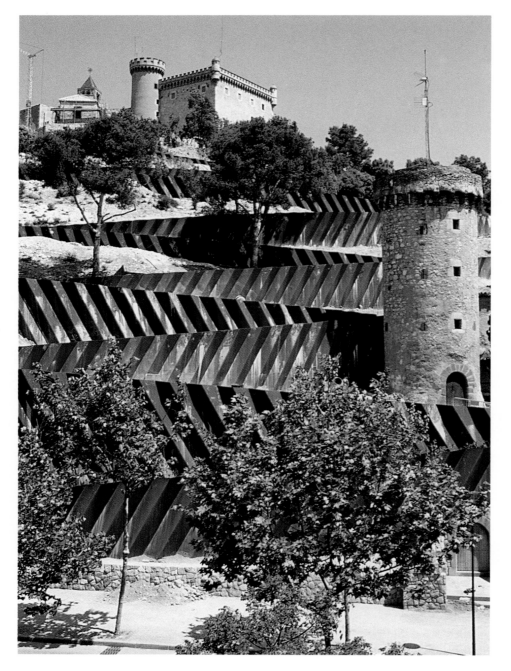

rectilinear mud-walled enclosures of the Egyptians, the pleasure grounds of the ancient Persians, and the peristyle gardens of the Greeks and Romans. The pattern was perpetuated in the cloister gardens of medieval monasteries and in Renaissance palace and manor-house gardens throughout civilized Europe. Finally, the traditional grid was still being used in the nineteenth and early twentieth century, when gardens were created in a potpourri of earlier European historical styles.

The organization of the ground plane is the basis of any garden or landscape design, whether formally or asymmetrically designed. A splendid example of the grid and its contemporary use can be seen in Kathryn Gustafson's design for Rights of Man Square at Evry, one of five new towns built near Paris during the 1970s. By the late 1980s the population of Evry had reached eighty thousand. The decision to build a new city square was an attempt by local and regional authorities to create a sense of unity in the rapidly growing city.

Gustafson, in collaboration with the architect Gerard Pas, won the competition for the design of the 2½-acre site in 1989. The organizers of the competition set the Rights of Man as the underlying motif for the design. Gustafson responded to Article II of the Rights of Man: freedom of expression. She created the square as a place for both public and private activity. There were to be municipal events and performances of music, dance, and drama. The square was also the town's platform where any of the inhabitants could give soap-box speeches. Finally, it was a pleasant place to meet friends or have a meal within the sight and sound of water and among plantings that brought the countryside into the newly built town.

By lowering the ground plane of the square, Gustafson created a definite boundary and removed the sunken space from the constant hurlyburly of the traffic that runs past. This was a brilliant stroke of design. The square is bounded by various important public and municipal buildings designed by noted French architects. The Autoroute du Sud

**Above** *An alternating rhythm and movement to right and left and from bottom to top of a hillside at Castelledefels near Barcelona, Spain, is established by steel-section retaining walls.*

**Far right** *The pure square has been used as the design module for the terrace of this San Francisco house, creating a strong sense of rhythm and movement.*

plants are all important. The combination of these features creates contrast, the single most important element in any design.

The first element in a garden or landscape upon which the architect or designer must focus is the ground plane, for all of the other elements in a design are governed by it. For at least two millennia—and longer if we include the Egyptian dynasties in the chronology—the ground plane of traditional gardens has been defined by a grid. This means that the site is squared off and divided into regular square or rectangular elements. The earliest example of gardens designed this way were the square or from Paris to the south runs down one side. The magnificent new cathedral and cloister of Saint Corbinien by Mario Botta, the Swiss-Italian architect, creates a central focus.

The main paving is made of pale gray Celtic granite overlaid with a grid of white granite. The grid is continuous, even when there are steps and ramps. These changes of level reflect each of the buildings surrounding the square. For example, the large granite staircase that leads down into the underground parking lot corresponds to the huge scale of the arc of Botta's cathedral.

A leading contemporary designer, Gustafson has revised the traditional arrangement of vertical and horizontal elements. She has organized them in ways that reflect her aesthetic and that of the late twentieth century. Their positions govern the contrasts of rhythm and movement intrinsic to the design.

The Dragon Basin is a superb raised pool of massive proportions made of green Brazilian granite. It is 415 feet long and varies from 16 to 25 feet wide. It is angled at one side so that it overlaps the grid ground plane and creates a visual connection between the town hall and chamber of commerce on one side of the square and the cathedral on the other.

Another design stroke relating to the rhythm of the layout is the division of the Dragon Basin into two sections linked by steps that provide access to two levels of the square. This means that a pedestrian has no need to walk the entire 415 feet of the basin in order to get from one point to another. This is an aesthetically pleasing and extremely efficient aspect of the rhythm and movement of the design.

Gustafson has designed two rectangles within the grid ground plan. The first is a rectangle of water that is called the Simmering Pool. A pattern of water jets churns up the surface of the water. Adjacent to it is a rectangular pavement area of a similar size. The area is patterned with holes from which 153 programmed jets can play vertically. The lighting of the Dragon Basin, the Simmering Pool, and the pavement adds another dimension to the rhythm and movement of Gustafson's design.

**Above** *In this design, which is entitled The Wave Field, a sense of movement is evoked by natural light and shadow and by people walking on the grassed earth waves or sheltering among them. The waves, which rise from ground level to a maximum of six feet, give rhythm to the piece. Maya Lin designed the site in 1995. It occupies an area of 675 square feet at the University of Michigan, Ann Arbor.*

**Right** *Low, undulating rolling land forms a contrast to the angled, parallel stone-edged canals in the Esso/Exxon headquarters garden near Paris.*

Another superb example of rhythm and movement can be found in the design for a raised terrace garden in San Francisco by Topher Delaney. Here the ground plane is paved in lines of white concrete pavers. The lines between them are made from dark green grass *Dichondra miscantha*. The verticals are provided by climbing plants against the white plaster perimeter walls. The other boundary walls are made of glass— but glass with a difference. They are double-skin glass panels ten feet high with an eight-inch space between the two sections.

At the bottom of the space, Delaney has placed strips of white neon to up-light the glass panels. Some of the panels fronting onto the terrace have been shot-blasted, and some of the rear panels are mirrored. The effect of this treatment is both beautiful and wonderfully elegant. It demonstrates the way in which the artist's or designer's imagination can elevate a contemporary material. Continuing the design module of the square, Delaney has created a square pool in which there are nine slightly raised square planters, all of which are planted with white zantedeschia lilies.

Site-generated references abound in Torres and Lapeña's design for Constitution Square on the edge of Gerona in northern Spain. The project was conceived by the municipal government of Gerona, which had decided in 1983 to dedicate a square to the new Constitution of Spain, ratified in 1978. A vaguely triangular site was chosen in a newly developed area of the city. It is bounded along one side by a major road, Gran Via de Jaume I, and a new building for the Bank of Spain, and on the other by an access ramp that leads to an underground parking lot and a school playground.

Torres and Lapeña decided initially that the square should become an urban garden, bringing a shard of nature into the heart of the city, just as a flowerpot brings a small token of nature into a house. Beautifully finished concrete was used to raise the level on one side of the square. The resulting ramps slope down to key into the sidewalks at their far end. Concrete was also used to define the edges of the site. Triangular, asymmetrical shapes and sections of the concrete were raised in places to serve as seating and to establish and emphasize the rhythm and movement of the triangular site.

The raised concrete on one side of the square serves as a wall for the ducting vents to service the underground parking lot. Torres and Lapeña have designed the entrance to the lot as a sharp, long triangle within part of another raised wall, making the entrance discreet, recessive, and at one with the rhythm and movement of the design.

# Time and Change

The elementary living entity would from its very beginning have had no more wish to change, if conditions remained the same; it would do no more than constantly repeat the same course of life. In the last resort, what has left its mark on the development of organisms must be the history of the earth we live in and its relation to the sun.

Sigmund Freud, *Beyond the Pleasure Principle*, 1921

The Age of Information has brought new meaning to the concepts of time and change. In our high-tech environment we are capable of keeping in touch with the reality of daily life all over the world. We also know more about history than ever before, and we have a much better idea of the relationship between time and change and the history of gardens.

Great gardens from the past have much to teach us. Their existence today is due to a deliberate policy of conservation. We will never know to what extent their past survival was dependent on chance. Some gardens have been cared for over many centuries by the same family. This is often the case in Italy, where it has been a good recipe for survival. Private citizens who take on the stewardship of a historic garden have often proved themselves to be saviors. The seventeenth-century gardens of Courances in France were rescued from dereliction in the twentieth century by the de Ganay family. Similarly, the long-abandoned estate of Désert de Retz was restored by Olivier Choppin de Janvry.

More recently, governments or charities have taken on the task of preserving our garden heritage. In Denmark there has been a concerted effort by the government to restore and conserve the formal gardens of the seventeenth-century Rosenberg Palace and the eighteenth-century gardens of Frederiksborg Castle and Fredensborg Palace. Similarly, in Japan the Great Stroll Garden of Katsura Imperial Villa Gardens has been preserved as far as possible in its original state, as have the Lake Garden of the Golden Pavilion and the Gravel Garden of the Silver Pavilion. Ryoan-ji Zen Garden and the other small but immensely important Zen Buddhist gardens of the subtemples in the Daitoku-ji precinct have also been preserved. In both Japan and Denmark, the garden landscape forms part of the traditions of art, architecture, and design that are intrinsic to society.

There are also international organizations in existence that are dedicated to the discovery and monitoring of historic gardens as well as identifying those of particular importance. The Benneton Foundation awards certain grants for the preservation of historic landscapes. Worlitz Park in Germany and Désert de Retz in France have both benefited in this way.

Other organizations are dedicated to the conservation of plants. Botanic Gardens Conservation International is based at Kew Gardens in London. It actively promotes plant conservation among its 500 member gardens across 110 countries. Many of the botanic gardens it sponsors are of great historic significance. Among its members are Padua and Pisa in Italy; Rio de Janeiro; Oxford, Cambridge, and the Chelsea Physic Garden in England.

*On the Making of Gardens*, published in 1909, is Sir George Sitwell's hymn to the great sixteenth-century gardens of Italy. It is a wonderful homage to time and change in the garden:

**Left and below** *One of the stunning earthworks by James Pierce in his "garden of history" in Maine. Earthwoman,* 1976, seen in three states *of time and change: clipped, at the summer solstice, and overgrown with grass and wild strawberries.*

Yet in truth such a garden as that of Lante is a world possession, and the builder of it a great poet who has influenced the life of thousands, putting them in touch with the greatness of the past, lifting their thoughts and aspirations to a higher level, revealing to them the light of their own soul, opening their eyes to the beauty of the world.

Architecture, the most unselfish of the arts, belongs to the passer-by, and every old house and garden in which the ideal has been sought is a gift to the nation, to be enjoyed by future generations who will learn from it more of history and art and philosophy than may be found in books.

Time combines with the weather to affect change in garden landscapes, whether they are contemporary or historic. The designers of contemporary site-generated or contextual landscapes make references to the effects of time in their designs. Geuze and West 8 in Holland; Desvigne & Dalnoky and Gustafson in France; Ariola and Piol, and Torres and Lapeña in Spain; and Stig Andersson in Denmark all use time and change to some degree in their designs. An outstanding example of this practice is found in the work of George Hargreaves. The central idea of Hargreaves Associates, based in Cambridge, Massachusetts, and San Francisco, is the connection between culture and environment, and between the land and the people. In the firm's designs, time and change become part of an ecological approach and the notion of sustainable landscape.

Hargreaves's design for Byxbee Park on the edge of San Francisco is a good example of the references to time and change in his designs. The landforms in the park are planted with indigenous grasses that change throughout the season. At Villa Zapu in the Napa Valley, he planted grass and wildflowers in serpentine patterns.

The ephemeral gardens of the Chelsea Flower Show have served to focus our minds on time and change. The Chanel garden in 1998 was a temporary example of a classical seventeenth-century French formal garden. It was installed over three weeks, seen by the public over five days, and dismantled in three days. This act of

defiance in the face of time contrasts with *Earthwoman* by James Pierce. *Earthwoman* is an example of land art based on ancient earthworks and built between 1970 and 1982. The piece is now biodegrading slowly.

Every aspect of the Chanel garden flew in the face of time. Tom Stuart-Smith, the British landscape architect responsible for the design, first met Karl Lagerfeld, design maestro for Chanel, in January 1997. At this early stage, it soon became evident that white camellias, in quantity, would be required, for they were Coco Chanel's favorite flower. It mattered not that camellias were only introduced to Europe in the nineteenth century, or that they bloom in late winter. Stuart-Smith did his best to dissuade the Chanel people from their choice, but to no avail. The fashion house already had its camellia line of products in process. Lagerfeld chose the name "Le Bosquet de Chanel" for the garden.

Time and change were certainly a problem for the camellias. The first batch was frost damaged. A replacement batch was housed first in a frostfree tunnel, then in a dark cold store, and finally under clear glass. By late May they were in full bloom.

On the Kennebec River near Hinckley, Maine, James Pierce makes earthworks on seventeen acres of meadow and woodland. His work has many primitive, elemental associations: "My medium is the landscape itself, its earth, rocks, and trees. I work in these materials because I feel their elemental power."

Pierce's *Stone Ship* makes references both to Viking burial and to Norse explorations of the Atlantic coast of North America. Stone boulders outline the ship on its raised earth platform. This is an explicit reference to the ancient burial rituals of the Vikings during the Bronze Age.

The Kiva is a ten-foot-wide subterranean chamber similar to those built by Native Americans for ceremonies. The spoil from the chamber was used to make the Triangular Redoubt and the Burial Mound. These are references to English and French settlements in the eighteenth century. Finally, the Turf Maze is linked to European gardens of the seventeenth century.

Pierce calls his earthworks "a garden of history." They represent his own perception of history and the meaning of time and change. He calls them "a relatively harmless means of satisfying desires for control, security, and immortality, while reliving the history of the race and discovering one's humanity in physical union with nature."

Sadly, Pierce is surrounded by changes that may eventually threaten his site. A paper mill has been built nearby and can be seen over the tops of the trees.

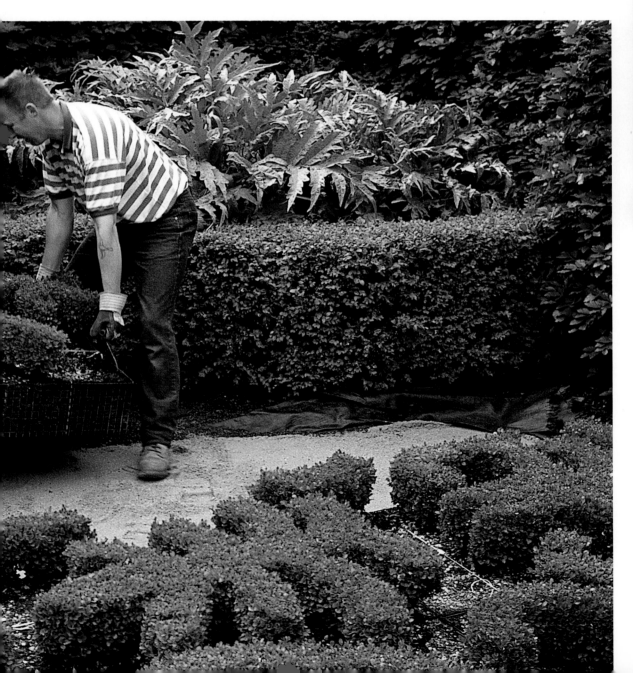

**Above and left** *Le Bosquet de Chanel garden, Chelsea Flower Show, London, 1998. Designed by Karl Lagerfeld and interpreted by Tom Stuart-Smith, it shows time and change at their most complex. The makings of the garden— its beech hedges, box bushes, Chanel Cs and all—were bought by an Irish woman for her own garden.*

New Elements

# Earth

I think earth is the material with most potential because it is the original source material . . . I found that, in using it, I could have a fairly complete vocabulary. It brought up all kinds of things about the prehistoric or preliterate past and referred to a lot of traditions about art that were more interesting than looking at works of art in the Louvre or the Metropolitan Museum.

Michael Heizer

Earth and land art have emerged as design forms truly unique to the gardens and landscapes of the latter part of the twentieth century. They are truly postmodern, but they have the most ancient antecedents.

Landscape architects and designers have been profoundly influenced by earth artists, who work directly with the land as their medium. Allied to this practice is a new awareness of the natural processes and uses of the earth. The imaginations of landscape designers worldwide have been fired by this approach, which they find useful on post-industrial sites.

In the late 1960s there were many earth artists. They were often painters or sculptors who recognized the ecological movement as an artistic antidote to the impact on the landscape of rampant late-nineteenth- and twentieth-century industrialization. These artists were also reacting against the increased hold of the international gallery owner/museum curator/art critic cabal on the art marketplace—not that its over-whelming grip has loosened any in the late 1990s. It should not be forgotten, however, that Virginia Dwan, a New York gallery owner, underwrote the first work by Heizer and Smithson, two of the most important land artists. Land art emerged from these two cultural and economic circumstances.

**Preceding pages** La Brume et Les Saules—*mist and willows with a difference, at Château de Chaumont-sur-Loire, the site of a unique international festival of garden and landscape. Willows were planted and woven into living sculptures, made mysterious by the autumn mist.*

**Left** La Terre en Marche (The Earth in Motion), *also at the Chaumont garden festival, is entered through a random grove of fiberglass rods. A gravel path ascends a spiral mound that offers views of the Loire River and the nearby Château de Chaumont. A serpentine, grassy beds, and white perennials create a contrast to the spiral.*

Land artists chose wild, untrammeled, and desolate places for their work (Utah and New Mexico), and in doing so, they seemed to be rediscovering what was known by our ancient ancestors: the interrelationships in the universe between space, infinite time, and art. Robert Smithson and Michael Heizer moved many tons of earth and rock in the deserts of Utah and Nevada to create massive earth sculptures that echo the earthworks and mounds of primitive and ancient peoples. Between 1969 and 1970, Heizer created *Double Negative* in the Nevada desert. It consisted of two cuts in a high, rocky tableland or mesa, which displaced 240,000 tons of earth. The cuts were 1,500 feet long, and each one was 30 feet wide and 50 feet deep. John Beardsley, whose books on land art and earthworks are the authoritative *ur*-texts on the subject, described *Double Negative* as "a consecrated space in which one experiences sensations of great distance, aloneness, and silence that inescapably recall the sublime."

Michael Heizer wrote about his discovery of "real space" in the desert in the following words: "The position of art as malleable barter-exchange item falters as the cumulative economic structure gluts. The museum and collections are stuffed, the floors are sagging, but real space exists." When Heizer talked to Beardsley, he said: "I don't care about landscape. I am a sculptor. Real estate is dirt, and dirt is material." He referred to the western landscape of the United States as "that kind of unraped, peaceful, religious space artists have always tried to put into their work."

**Right** *Earth design at Wadi Rayrn in Egypt. This was the result of a project given to French landscape architecture students in 1995. They were briefed to create a design without water or plants and supplied with a length of rope and two boards. The rest was left to their imaginations.*

**Below** *An earthwork interpretation in Maine of Janus, the Roman god of two faces. Here he has four eyes and four noses. He can be read from any perspective. The summer solstice sun rises through one of his eyes.*

*Double Negative* was not portable art merchandise. Perhaps more important still, it was not sculpture in the traditional sense, since it was not a constructed form or a mass: it was a sculpture from the space created in the two giant cuts in the earth of the mesa. Despite these distinctions, photographs of Heizer's earthworks do change hands for ready money in art galleries across the world.

In this section on earth, we will focus on the use of the spiral. This is both because it has caught our interest as designers and writers, and because it has inspired a large number of contemporary landscape architects and designers whose projects span a wide range of designs.

The spiral has been "rediscovered" in the last twenty years as a landform. It was first made, along with other primitive marks such as the circle, the serpentine, and the zigzag, some say, seventeen thousand years ago, when it was incised into bone tools and weapons and painted on cave walls. We can still see these primary, primitive shapes much later in the stone and wood henges, or circles, of western Europe, in the giant stone outlines of the Nazca in Peru, in the huge snake and water-spider earthworks of the Missouri and Mississippi river valleys of middle North America, and in the labyrinths of earth, stone, and sod that are found in all cultures of the world over many millennia.

We see the use of these primitive shapes by artists and landscape architects in the late twentieth century as part of a splendid, contemporary leap of the imagination. They represent a grand historical

**Below** *Large sculpted earth shapes below the Tokio Marine Oyama Training Center, Tochigi prefecture, Japan. The forms are enhanced by lines of grass and gravel referring to ancient farming methods and contemporary abstract painting.*

trajectory back over the sweep of garden history. The starting point is the current English granny-gardener, with a cottage or manor-house formal plan and informal planting inspired by Hidcote, Sissinghurst, Arts and Crafts, Robinson, and Jekyll. We refer to this as the "chintz slipcovers inside and herbaceous borders outside" school of design. The arc then spans the Victorian and American Beaux-Arts historical pastiche, the Italianate landscape or "landskip" Capability Brown style, Versailles style, the Italian Renaissance style based on villa gardens of Rome and Greece, the enclosed gardens and landscapes of Persia and Egypt, and finally, over millennia of unknown and undocumented garden history, the cave dweller. The labyrinth, circle, zigzag, serpentine, and spiral still have resonance today. Their use reconnects contemporary design to the earth.

The creation of *Spiral Jetty* by Robert Smithson

**Below** Spring Tide on Earth *is an earth, sod, and Cor-Ten steel construction in Belgium.*

The spiral is a shape widely used in contemporary landscapes. Its genesis is universal, ancient, and arithmetical. In nature, the living mathematics of the spiral can be seen in the spirals of the ammonite and the nautilus. Some of the arithmetic and geometric precedents of the shape are the spiral of Archimedes and the spiral of the golden section, and taken from it are the moldings of classical architecture—ogee, astragal, cyma recta, and ovolo. Plant and flower spiral formations were discovered by the thirteenth-century Italian mathematician Leonardo of Pisa, known as Fibonacci. The Fibonacci series of numbers follows an arithmetic sequence that can be found in the seed and leaf formations of plants. Equally profound and exciting are the Fibonacci spirals found in the cross section of the growing tip of a plant shoot or generative spiral: the primordia. Fibonacci's thirteenth-century theories, taken from Hindu-Arabic texts on the spiral nature of plants, were borne out by the epic twentieth-century discovery of the spiral of DNA by Crick and Watson at Cambridge.

There are many other examples of contemporary spiral landforms. One of them can be found in the Egyptian desert at El Ghouna near the Red Sea. Desert Breath consists of two interlocking spirals of precise positive and negative conical volumes of sand, ascending in height and descending in depth from the common center of a circular pool one hundred feet in diameter. In Scotland, Charles Jencks has designed a fifty-foot-high grassed earthwork that he refers to variously as "a snail," "a mound," and "a mount." At Villa Zapu in the northern end of California's Napa Valley, George Hargreaves designed a pair of spiral bands of wild grass and flowers around a mound. The spirals progressively unfurl into serpentines, which flow toward, and then underpin, the rest of the garden and the house.

was a very significant moment in the history of land art. The primitive spiral made of earth, black basalt, and limestone was built out from the shore into the waters of the Great Salt Lake in 1970. It is 1,500 feet long. Smithson was initially attracted to the site because it was covered in industrial junk and abandoned vehicles left over from a failed oil-extraction project. He believed that both this project and the large-scale earth art projects he made from reclaimed mine sites in Ohio and Colorado made a positive statement: "Art can become a physical resource that mediates between the ecologist and the industrialist."

The spiral form of salt crystals viewed under a microscope was a major source of inspiration for *Spiral Jetty*. Smithson was also very taken by a microorganism in the lake that colors the water dark pink. His giant, macro, spiral form came from a minute microanalysis of an aspect of the lake's composition. After twenty-eight years, the earth and rocks of the jetty that once stuck out of the water of the lake are now beginning to be submerged. It has become what Smithson predicted: "matter collapsing into the lake mirrored in the shape of a spiral."

**Center** *Lower Manhattan's Jacob Javits Plaza was a featureless space improved originally by Richard Serra's* Tilted Arc *sculpture. This proved too controversial and was removed. In 1997 this new design was created. It consists of "topiary" made from misting grassed hemispheres, 6 feet high, which cool the air for office workers relaxing on the swirling, double-sided benches.*

**Below** *Double spirals of earth and grass for the Cité des Arts, Paris, 1991, recall the* parterres de broiderie *of French formal gardens. Here the parterres are realized as twentieth-century sculptured Land Art.*

# Water

"What pleases me most in these new fountains," said Claudio Tolomei, "is the variety of ways with which they guide water, turn it, lead it, break it, make it rise and fall." This sixteenth-century account of Roman fountains and decorative waterworks would do very nicely to describe the amazing variety of contemporary water features and incidents in gardens and landscapes four hundred years later.

The high-tech water engineering that has been made available to contemporary garden and landscape designers over the past twenty-five years would, in its magical effects and diverse configurations, dazzle Signore Tolomei. He would be amazed by the artificial

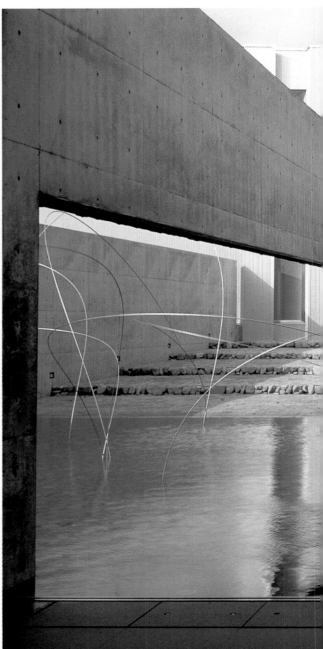

# The thing about water is that it can do what nothing else can do.   Daniel Urban Kiley

fog that can be created at the flick of a switch connected to some very expensive engineering and computer technology.

Water has been praised and extolled throughout history on account of the practical and aesthetic pleasures that it offers. In gardens and landscapes, water is the most mutable design element, and now it is also the most manageable. Perhaps it is true to say that water is the most sensuous element in the garden and often the most visually exciting. It can either be the gentlest or the most dramatic part of the design, whether it is found in the smallest of private gardens or the largest public display. Wind, wildlife,

and humans are the only other capricious and changeable participants in a garden scene.

In Europe, the distinction between the uses of water in the north and south has always been determined by geography and climate. In regions north of the olive tree cordon in upper Provence, there is a preponderance of both natural and human-made lakes, pools, and ponds that act as wonderful, dark mirrors to draw down the sky and clouds. Perhaps the cooler, grayer, rainier skies of the north need fewer fountain jets.

The countries where the olive flourishes lie below that invisible geographical line that northern Europeans love to cross in order to find the heat, the

**Far left** *In the Crystal Garden Lobby, Sea Hawk Hotel and Resort, Fukuoka, Japan, there are fifty-foot-high waterfalls made from serpentine ribbons of glass. When the water is turned off, the glass ribbons become giant sculptures.*

**Below** *The ground plane of the still pool in Arata Isozaki's Nagi Museum of Contemporary Art is the setting for a stainless-steel sculpture by Aiko Miyawaki.*

sea, and the sand. Here, the long, hot days of the Mediterranean summer inspire gardens containing water in every possible form. Waterfalls, sprays, and splashes indulge the senses of both sight and sound.

In 1989 we visited forty-five Italian gardens between Lake Maggiore and Naples. We saw every possible variation on the use of water, from the still nymphaeum pool of the Villa Barbaro near Venice to the greatest conflation and variety of Renaissance waterworks at the Villa d'Este, east of Rome. Here we recovered from the heat in the black shade of a giant and mythic cypress tree, seeing and listening to the wonderfully refreshing play of Pirro Ligorio's fountains.

designed for Louis XIV on the flat ground below the palace of Versailles would have played continuously. As it was, Le Nôtre depended on a complex set of hand signals between the garden boys hidden in the hedges throughout the garden.

Today, electronic and digitally programmed computers, micropiping and jets, fiber-optic lighting, and even artificial fog, created by water atomized under high pressure, are all available to garden and landscape designers. Another major technical improvement in the use of water has come from the development of polymer and butyl membrane liners for waterproofing pools and lakes, enabling reservoirs to be made on a much larger scale, and on terrain usually considered unsatisfactory. This has meant large lakes and reservoirs can be created on desert sites in the countries of the Middle East. Used to contain both fresh and salt water, they service the needs of the population and the newly constructed palace gardens of the ruling class.

Liners have replaced the traditional puddling mode of waterproofing, when workers would stamp in a mixture of heavy clay and sand to make the

**Below** *Sphagnum moss, wire mesh, and steam are the main elements of the mysterious* Puffing Mosses *set in a pool at Stockholm's annual Rosendal garden show in 1998.*

**Right** *The Water Garden jets at night in* Fragments of Garden History, *a public park at Terrasson-La-Villedieu, France.*

Ippolito d'Este, the cardinal who was Ligorio's patron, ordered his workmen to alter the course of the nearby River Aniene so a limitless head of water was provided to gravity-feed Ligorio's extensive and magical designs. Where are such patrons of garden design today?

If only today's advanced water engineering had been available to André Le Nôtre in seventeenth-century France. Then the beautiful fountains he impermeable lining of ponds, lakes, embankments, and canals. When the eighteenth-century Moon Ponds at Studley Royal in northern England were drained, some workers' footprints were found intact.

Although waterproof liners are widely used today, there are some situations in which traditional puddling is more effective. We puddled the 1½-acre lake that we created in 1990 on the Elton John estate. The puddling was not done with the stamping feet of our workers, however, but with the front buckets of large earth-moving equipment that worked a layer of clay onto the bottom and sides of the lake area.

Water can be used to create a vast variety of effects. It can be incredibly subtle, as in the almost impercep-tible sheen that spreads serenely down both the rough and the cut faces of a large rock that Isamu Noguchi placed in the Japanese wing of the Metropolitan Museum of Art, New York. An exquisite murmuring sound comes from the water hitting the surface of the reservoir under the boulder. The surrounding area is masked by pebbles.

The low, vigorous waterfalls in Fountain Plaza, Dallas, Texas, were designed by Daniel Urban Kiley. He set two hundred mature swamp cypresses in circular planters among the waterfalls and water jets, creating a refreshing environment for workers from the adjacent sixty-story I. M. Pei office building and for passersby escaping the relentless heat of the midday sun. The flow of water for the falls and jets is controlled by a complex set of computers.

The Kiley garden is an excellent example of the use in large public gardens and landscapes of "gray" or recycled, non-potable water in place of fresh water, a natural resource that is becoming more and more precious. "Gray water" is the sane and sensible path toward the conservation of a diminishing natural resource.

**Below** *Technically advanced pumps activate this* carrousel d'eau, *an installation built in a French garden in 1996. The still water of the central pool contrasts with the waves, bubbles, and ripples created by the various pumps.*

Some twentieth-century landscape designers and architects have had a great influence on the way water is used in contemporary gardens and landscapes. Alvar Aalto, the great Finnish architect, designed the first free-form, curvilinear swimming pool for the Villa Mairea outside Helsinki. Thomas Church, the innovator of the California style of garden design, was inspired by Aalto's designs and imported his distinctive stools, chairs, and vases to San Francisco. We think that Church's pool at El Novillero near Sonoma was directly inspired by Aalto's pool at Villa Mairea. Church's beautiful design for the pool and garden are counted as twentieth-century masterpieces. When seen from a nearby hilltop, the shape of the pool echoes the distant, curving salt marshes below the northern reaches of San Francisco Bay. The design of Church's pool was picked up by various magazines—hence the endless, bright blue, kidney-shaped swimming pools that proliferated in backyards all over southern California.

Frank Lloyd Wright, with his design for Fallingwater at Bear Run, Pennsylvania, is another architect who has had a profound influence on future generations of landscape architects, designers, and the other environmental professions. Fallingwater is brilliantly sited. It seems to be interwoven with the trees, the rocks, the stream, and its waterfall. From a distance, the strong horizontals of the house are in perfect harmony with the landscape elements. If only the clients had followed Wright's suggestion that the horizontals of the main structure should be covered in a dull-colored gold leaf. Then the house would have become truly at one with the golden color of the autumn leaves.

Fallingwater was Wright's greatest achievement and most original contribution to architecture. Here he demonstrated his new concept of space by creating rooms that overlap both vertically and horizontally. He made subtle use of natural lighting and provided woodland or stream views from every room. Rooms were defined by function, and there was a constant interplay between indoors and outdoors, all underpinned at Fallingwater by the constant sound of the stream from the waterfalls beneath the house.

Carlo Scarpa, the legendary Italian modernist

architect, had a profound influence on landscape architects and designers. He created quiet, subtle planes of water in the form of shallow pools adjacent to his private houses and in the courtyards of his public buildings. Scarpa was a follower of Frank Lloyd Wright's architectural style rather than the prevailing International Style of Mies van der Rohe. The American and German architects' antithetical views represented a cultural divide similar to the division between Matisse and Picasso. In each instance, the division is still debated by "culture vultures" on both sides of the Atlantic.

Scarpa's shallow pools of water reflect and soften the buildings. Some examples are important to note. On the garden side of the Casa Veritti in Udine, the arc edge of the pool is a variation on the curved roof of the house; the arcs contrast with the triangular shape of the double-height glass walls of the main room. The shallow, rhomboid-shaped pool at the Villa Ottolenghi is fed from the water running off the roof. In the courtyard of the Palazzo Querini Stampalia, Venice, he created a maze of low square and rectangular pools that feed into a central double square pool in which white water lilies grow.

Scarpa's masterpiece is the Brion Family Cemetery, Treviso. Here his shallow water incidents lead the visitor inside the boundaries of the cemetery. A long, formalized rill diminishes in width as it focuses on the

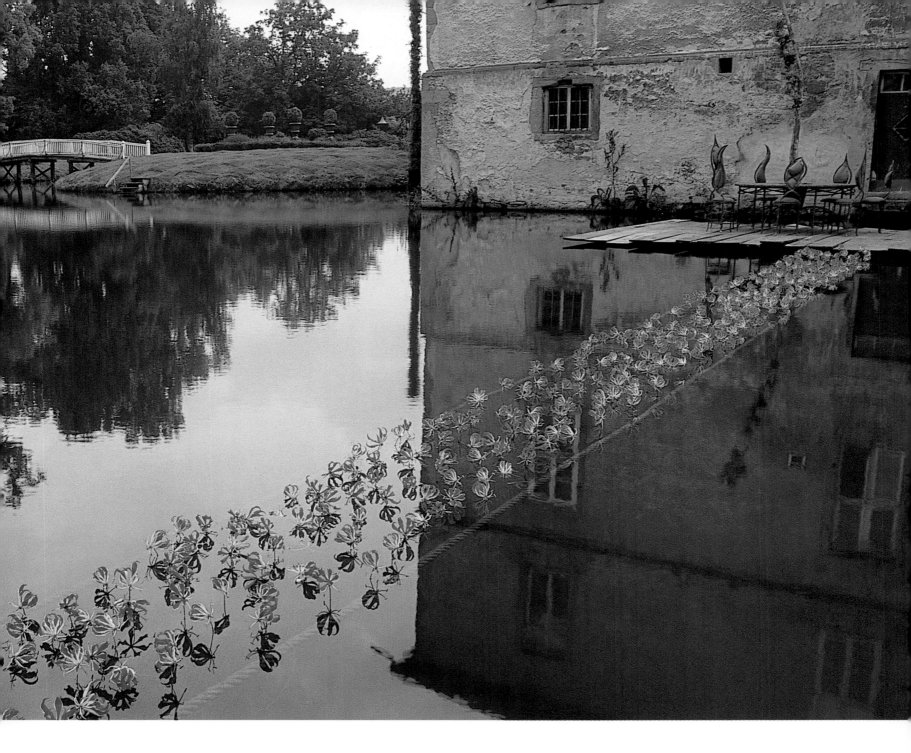

two sarcophagi under their protective arch. The family chapel sits on the diagonal in a low square pool. Water lilies embrace its sides. The modest water incidents strike a correct, recessive note in the cemetery.

Luis Barragán makes water fall from narrow spouts at the ends of rectangular planar walls stuccoed in the brightest Mexican bougainvillea colors. Barragán was much inspired by the traditional wooden aqueducts that were created to carry water over the villages of his native Guadalajara. One of his minimalist masterworks is the horse trough he designed between 1958 and 1962 at Las Arboledas, near Mexico City. Here he employed the simplest of materials: the water was in a raised trough. At one

end there were two rectangular walls, one white to gather the shadows from the grove of tall eucalyptus trees, and one blue to suggest distance, thus achieving a minimalist grandeur. Barragán has had a potent and continuous influence on landscape architects and designers in the United States, Europe, and even as far away as Australia. His style is now being carried forward by the architect Ricardo Legorreta.

Noguchi was also a master in the use of water. His skill is particularly evident in his smaller-scale court-yards: the plaza of Chase Manhattan Bank, New York City; *California Scenario,* Costa Mesa, California; and the Beinecke Rare Book and Manuscript Library, Yale University, New Haven, Connecticut.

**Above** *The mirrored water of the moat of Schloss Hunnefeld, Bad Essen, Osnabruck, Germany, is the site of a floating minimalist installation created by Tage Andersen, the noted Danish florist, for the castle's 850th anniversary.*

**Left** *A courtyard garden in Santa Fe, New Mexico, seen in winter. It has a contemporary black granite pool and a waterfall inspired by the traditions of the Southwest.*

# Sculpture

My intention is not to improve on nature but to know it
—not as a spectator but as a participant. I do not wish to
mimic nature, but to draw on the energy that drives it so
that it drives my work also. My art is unmistakably the work
of a person—I would not want it to be otherwise—it
celebrates my human nature and a need to be physically
and spiritually bound to the earth.

Andy Goldsworthy

**Right**  *Nature and culture "dance" into the twenty-first century. An evergreen holm oak and a concrete triangle assemblage by Mauro Staccioli at the Museum of Contemporary Art, Tortoli, Italy.*

**Below**  *Iron, water, and bark are juxtaposed, giving wonderful reflections of the sky and the surrounding landscape.*

Sculpture is no longer sited as a single focal point or "eye-catcher" in contemporary gardens and landscapes. It is either integrated into a garden or landscape or the concept for its creation arises directly from its situation. Another characteristic that is peculiar to contemporary sculpture is the loss of its religious and political connotations. During the 1990s landscape architects and designers were drawn to works of sculpture inspired directly by nature. These pieces had a sense of belonging to a specific garden or landscape. In other words, they were site-specific, site-generated sculptures as opposed to works inspired by a different historical period and a different culture and set of beliefs.

The twentieth century has been unique in its exploration of new designs and materials for sculpture and the use to which these sculptures are put. Picasso, Matisse, Arp, Miró, de Kooning, and Calder created sculpture that was, for the most part, portable. Even the large pieces for public display could be moved—with a crane, in some cases.

Portability is no longer relevant to leading-edge contemporary sculptors. Their work is either on such a huge scale, or made of such fragile natural materials, that the portable aspect is null and void. The portable, saleable record of their work, which has become the "work of sculpture," is either the concept sketch or a photo of the finished work. Some major examples from the 1970s and 1980s are Christo and Jeanne-Claude wrapping the Reichstag in Berlin with tensile material, or *The Umbrellas*, seven thousand yellow tensile umbrellas "intervening" in long lines through the landscape north of San Francisco.

The beauty and originality of work using natural objects has aroused a deep interest in the natural landscape. Andy Goldsworthy, with his "found" materials of twigs, ice, sand, and clay, and his leaf patterns on trees and in still pools, is at the forefront of this movement, as is Richard Long with his arrangements of "found" rocks and flowers. Work of this kind has had an enormous influence on garden and landscape designers worldwide.

Goldsworthy, in his book *Touching North,* refers to one of the most ephemeral of his sculptures:

Its energy is made visible in ice and snow. When I work with winter I work with the North. The further North I go the stronger its presence. I want to follow North to its source—to try and come to terms with it—in the same way I work with a leaf under the tree from which it fell. I want to understand the nature of North as a whole. Unlike the summit of a mountain, the North Pole has no distinctive feature to tell you are there—there is no land—only snow and ice. There is little difference between the Pole and the surrounding five hundred miles. It is more of a feeling than a place. It belongs to no one—it is the earth's common—an ever-changing landscape in which whatever I make will soon disappear.

The twentieth century has also seen a change in the public display of sculpture. We now have temporary, traveling exhibitions in public parks, sculpture parks with permanent collections, and, most important of all, the development of land, earth, and environmental art, based on the concept of the site generated.

*Right  Christo and Jeanne-Claude's Wrapped Trees, Fondation Beyeler and Berower Park, Riehen, Switzerland, 1997–98: the latest project of artists who have been working on, among other things, wrapping trees for thirty-two years. Here 178 trees have been wrapped in 590,000 square feet of woven polyester fabric and fourteen miles of rope.*

*Below  Secret Life IV, 1998, by Peter Randall-Page at Wenlock Priory, Shropshire, England. Sir Roy Strong says that Randall-Page "stands at the end of the line which stretches back to Celtic crosses and down to William Morris."*

Contemporary landscape architects and designers are concerned with sculpture inspired by nature that has a sense of belonging to its natural surroundings. In other words, they prefer the site generated and tend to avoid works that are the product of a different historical period. This is very different from the position taken by practitioners in the past, when garden artifacts were seen as a statement of wealth. In contemporary gardens, sculpture is an integrated part of the design.

Public sculpture gardens began to be made in the early twentieth century in Scandinavia. Gustav Vigeland made a highly personal sculpture garden on an island in a fjord near Oslo. It is famous for its amazing pillar sculpture of writhing bodies. In Stockholm, the Carl Milles Garden is on a series of terraces with pools and fountains, on which light and airy sculptures stand at various levels, silhouetted against the Swedish skies.

Scandinavia's largest public sculpture garden is at the Louisiana Museum, nineteen miles north of Copenhagen. It is one of the earliest and most successful combinations of landscape, architecture, painting, and sculpture. Its holdings of international modern art rank with the major collections elsewhere in the world, such as the Tate Gallery in London. The garden is on the site of a nineteenth-century manor to which glass and wood corridor galleries have been added, adjacent to the wooded boundaries of the site. The sculptures are set within the woods; some are out in the open, and others are situated within a variety of enclosures that are connected by carefully designed paths. In 1986 the patrons of the museum added *The Gate in the Gorge*, a site-generated sculpture by Richard Serra, and in 1994 Per Kirkeby's untitled brick sculpture.

The Kröller-Müller Museum in the Netherlands was built in 1961 on a one-hundred-acre site in a former hunting forest. Again, glass-walled galleries have been used to divide the formal approach to the museum from the more irregular woodland clearing and the lake. The sculpture is placed between the open views and the more enclosed wooded areas of the site.

The Kröller-Müller and Louisiana Museums have been the models for sculpture parks in many different countries on diverse sites, often covering large areas. In New York State, the Storm King Art Center, which is north of New York City, covers two hundred acres. In Great Britain, the Welsh Sculpture Park at Magram has a stunning 880-acre site that includes an Iron Age fort and wooded parkland with lakes and formal gardens close to the museum. On the former Bretton Hall estate in Yorkshire, the sculpture park covers

**Above** *The Star of David Pavilion, 1991–96, by Dan Graham in the moat of Schloss Buchberg, Austria. Sculpture, glass architecture, and two-way mirrors magically transmute the landscape, brilliantly fooling the senses.*

260 acres. These large landscape sites demand sculpture on a larger scale to harmonize with the longer views.

Garden or courtyard sites are more harmonious for the display of smaller-scale sculpture. Noguchi's courtyard masterpiece for the Beinecke Rare Book and Manuscript Library, Yale University, New Haven, Connecticut, and his sculpture gardens for Chase Manhattan Bank, New York City, along with his design at the IBM Headquarters in New York State, are but three of these. Also in New York City is the exquisite garden for twentieth-century sculpture of the Museum of Modern Art designed by Philip Johnson and James Fanning.

In Great Britain, two important twentieth-century sculptors have created landscape or garden settings for their work. The first is Dame Barbara Hepworth in St. Ives, Cornwall, and the other is Sir Henry Moore at Much Haddam in Hertfordshire.

There are three important late-twentieth-century private gardens in Great Britain that must be noted for their sculpture. The first is in the Pentland hills south of Edinburgh. Here the poet Ian Hamilton Finlay has made what some critics describe as the most original garden created in Britain since 1945. Sculpture is used to make Finlay's philosophical and polemical points about antiquity and the revolutionary nature of the human spirit. In Hertfordshire, the architect Sir Frank Gibberd created a sculpture garden of "found" architectural objects and also sited sculptures by contemporary British sculptors whom he had encouraged during the 1960s and 1970s. Similarly, Lord Carrington's interest in contemporary sculptors has made his garden in Buckinghamshire into a showcase for the new generation of sculptors in the 1980s and 1990s. The collection includes splendid, large-scale stone acorns, pine cones, and fruit pieces by Peter Randall-Page.

Site-generated sculpture collections have emerged all over Europe and the United States over the past twenty years. In Europe, Grizedale in Cumbria is particularly important, as is Domaine de Kerguennec near Josselin in Brittany, France, and Villa Celle near

Florence in Italy. At the Abington Arts Center, Pennsylvania, there is a fascinating permanent installation called "A Reclamation Garden" by Winifred Lutz. She has been making her name as an artist working in both paper and wood, and here she is asking and answering contemporary questions to do with art versus nature, culture versus nature, and the permanence of the garden.

Lutz shapes her installations from the branches and twigs of the woodland near the arts center. Names emerge from the shapes she creates: *The Deadfall Dome*, *The Red Oak Portal*, *The Impact Zone;* all of these are impermanent and give the illusion of being naturally formed. The only permanent shape is the fifteen-foot stone tower, which is definitely human-made and will have a longer life than the installations made from the "found" woodland materials.

These modest woodland site-generated sculptures are not the vast bulldozer-made signs on the earth made by Michael Heizer or Robert Smithson in the 1960s and 1970s. However, they pose a similar set of questions about being and nonbeing, existence and non-existence.

**Above** *Section of a spiral of standing stones from the Mist Garden created in France, 1998. The spiral is punctuated by spaces, or "windows," onto the surrounding landscape. Mist animates ammonite forms in stone slabs and also nurtures the ferns planted among them.*

**Far left** *By the pond in the Hannah Peschar Sculpture Garden, Surrey, England, are these figures made from galvanized steel mesh by British sculptor David Begbie. The female is called* Limber, *made in 1998, and the male is* Lean, *made in 1996.*

## Case Studies

# Robert Irwin

## Lower Central Garden, The Getty Center, Los Angeles, California

"A sculpture in the form of a garden aspiring to be art." This became Robert Irwin's mantra when he was working on his design for the Lower Central Garden of the Getty Center. The Getty garden is a wonderful example of site-generated design—a concept that has inspired some of the most creative landscape architects and garden designers in the United States, France, Holland, and Spain. The shapes and forms of the design are drawn from within the site, rather than being imposed upon it in the traditional way. In Irwin's own words, this amounts to "playing it as it lays."

As we drove up the San Diego Freeway on Interstate 405 from Long Beach, we saw a striking group of buildings perched on the point of an escarpment above the Sepulveda Pass. At first we thought that they might be a 1950s Veterans' Administration hospital, but as we got nearer, we realized that it could only be the Getty Center, designed by Richard Meier. It is a pity the community of Brentwood residents above and below the complex was so intransigent about the project. The draconian restrictions they imposed prevented Meier from using his characteristic white metal panels; they had to be painted off-white. The reflective white metal contrasting with the stone would have been superb, a splendid design opportunity lost.

The Getty is the richest center of art in the world. Thirteen years in the making, it covers 110 acres high above Los Angeles. On a clear day, Catalina Island in the Pacific is visible to the west and Mount Baldy to the east. Meier's hilltop campus, which was built at a cost of $1 billion, consists of the J. Paul Getty Museum (fifty-four galleries) and five cultural institutes, including an auditorium.

**Far right** *Robert Irwin's "trees" designed for the plaza of the Lower Central Garden of the Getty Center. Made from concrete reinforcing rods, the trees provide vertical interest and make excellent climbing frames for bougainvillea.*

## GARDEN STATISTICS

**Client:** The Getty Center

**Budget:** $8.5 million

**Designer:** Robert Irwin

**Area:** 3½ acres

**Climate:** Southern Californian

**Soil type:** Sandy topsoil

**Aspect:** West

**Date of completion:** 1997

**Number of gardeners:** 5

Along with the beige metal panels, the buildings are faced in sand-colored travertine, cut from ancient quarries near Rome. Some thirty-seven thousand tons of this stone were used.

The Getty board, which should be eternally thanked for its vision, wanted "an artist's sensibility" to be applied to the design of the lower gardens. Robert Irwin was appointed to design the Lower Central Garden on the 3½-acre west-facing slope of a natural canyon below the buildings.

This is said to have caused Meier no end of anguish. His first reaction was to demand a thirty-foot-wide *cordon aesthetique* of lawn between his buildings and the edge of the valley where the garden was to be. When telling us about this, Irwin's tone of voice was similar to that of a patient Montessori kindergarten school teacher: "It was hard for him to have someone else paint on his canvas." We presume that Meier did not want any trees and shrubs to blur the mathematical rigor of his buildings.

Irwin's working life as a leading American artist is also a précis of modern art in the latter half of the twentieth century. It begins with his paintings as an Abstract Expressionist in the 1950s. In the late 1960s he chucked his art supplies and began his journey from what he calls "ground zero" as another kind of artist. He investigated art and technology, installation art, light-and-space Art, Los Angeles "Look" art, and public art. These different art forms

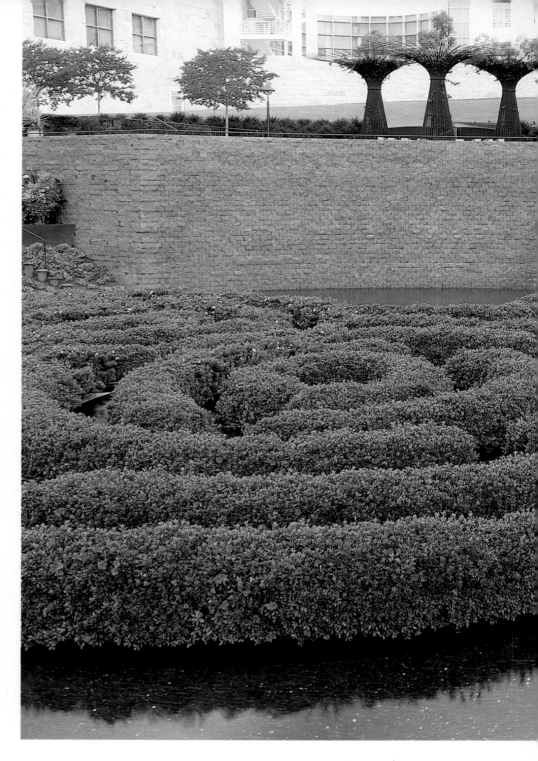

**Above** *The dramatic, Mogul-inspired waterfall feeds into a circular pool on which pink and red azaleas create an ancient maze pattern.*

**Left** *An aerial view of Richard Meier's Getty Center. The museum is on the right, and the art history center, encompassing Robert Irwin's design, is on the left.*

**Above** *Irwin's early colored presentation plan of the Lower Central Garden reveals its giant stem and flower form.*

**Below** *Irwin's model delineates the circle, maze, serpentine, and zigzag, the major design elements of the garden.*

**Above** *Irwin went to Montana and South Dakota to select the rocks for the serpentine stream. He arranged them down the center of the original canyon site to orchestrate the sound of the running water and create the maximum visual impact.*

**Above right** *Teak benches on the stone path provide a place to enjoy the sound of water and the shade of the plane trees.*

can all be described as either site generated, or site-conditioned.

With the Getty project, Irwin moved from site-generated projects inside buildings to an exterior site. When he accepted the challenge, he stated that he was not a gardener. However, we consider the Lower Central Garden a masterpiece of site-generated landscape design. Its main elements have emerged from Irwin's deep analysis of the site (his main aim was to restore and adapt to the canyon site), but they also reflect some of the most important metaphors in garden history. The design incorporates the serpentine, the zigzag, a Japanese reverence for the placing of stones, the formal allée, the circle, the bosque, the labyrinth, the terrace, viewing points, and a unique and expressive use of plants. And viewed from above, the circle of terraces, with the pool with labyrinth of azaleas, becomes a splendid parterre. The configuration of the circle and water course aerially hallucinate into a giant flower and stem.

Irwin has designed a central serpentine line of water down the slope that is divided by a wonderful zigzag stone path. This is a perfect example both of Irwin "playing it as it lays" and of the site-generated. In his original plan the paths were straight down the sides of the water course. Irwin was then confronted by the Los Angeles ordinance on wheelchair access. This meant adapting the path to a zigzag ramp, yet another design stroke among the many in this garden. Where the triangular sides of the ramp meet the lawn area, they are retained with upstands of Cor-Ten steel. Since the Getty Center is open two nights a week, Irwin designed tall standard lights to illuminate the ramp. When seen from above, the lamps outline the form of the serpentine and circular elements of the garden and, as Irwin puts it, provide "a drawing of the garden."

Between each crossing of the zigzag ramp, Irwin has placed rocks he selected himself in Montana and South Dakota. These are arranged so they "tune" the water to different decibels at each level of the garden. At the first level the water is only heard, not seen, under the rocks. As one descends the slope, the water is visible and the sound is more pronounced. It reaches a climactic roar as it falls from the fifty-foot waterfall into the pool at the bottom of the plan. The rough boulders get smaller and more ordered, until at the plaza the water course has become a shallow, fast-running channel lined with a diamond pattern of stone setts and narrow steps, allowing visitors to step down to the stream's edge. This is Irwin's variation on the Persian

**Right** *Exquisite small stone setts on the stream bed contrast with large boulders and rocks. The main zigzag path of stone changes to teak bridges over the stream.*

and Mogul chuddar waterfall, which is angled and stepped to give more sound and glitter to the water as it falls. On the edge of the pool, above the waterfall, there is a bronze arc, which acts as a safety balustrade and a handrail. It also looks like a stylized setting sun, giving an Art Deco reference to Hollywood in the 1920s and 1930s—just one more example of Irwin's sensitive and visionary grasp of design.

The planting is carefully calibrated from the top to the very bottom of the water course. Under the plane trees at the top, gray-leaved plants predominate. Midway down the slope the leaf colors turn to red, purple, and dark green. Irwin uses these dark colors to contrast with the pale walls of Meier's stone and metal buildings. Finally, at the lowest level, the plants are pale green with yellow flowers. When questioned by members of the more conventional landscape architect community about his diverse selection of plants, the high levels of maintenance they would require, and their mutability, Irwin replied: "Let's assume this garden is art." He believes that the Getty should curate the garden just as it does the art objects in the museum.

The plaza is a generous, open space, a striking contrast to the serpentine water course, the zigzag ramp, and the interlaced labyrinths of azaleas that embrace the pool and appear to be floating on the water. During the flowering season, one gardener has

the sole duty of plucking off the spent azalea blossoms. Irwin has designed a ladder down to the pool specifically for this purpose.

The lower tiers of shallow, amphitheater terraces above the pool are planted with hundreds of species of perennial and annual plants and encircled with crape myrtles. Irwin chose the myrtles for their deciduous nature, since he believes that "bareness is beautiful." On the top tier of the amphitheater are serried ranks of grass. These look wonderful all year; even when they have been cut back in the winter, they have attractive, sculptural shapes.

Where the ramp enters the plaza, there are two trios of monumental, bronzed "tree" shapes. Each one is twelve feet high and made of concrete reinforcing rods. The structures will eventually be clothed in *Bougainvillea* 'Tahitian Dawn.' Their crucial role now as tall, arboreal shapes will be transferred to the allée of London planes (*Platanus acerifolia* 'Yarwood') on either side of the water course.

**Above** *The zigzag paths, required for access by the disabled, made the final design stronger. Cor-Ten steel upstands retain the earth of the flowerbeds and support bronze handrails.*

**Left** *Honeysuckle, roses, and heliotrope combine with many other scented plants to create an omnium-gatherum of herbaceous and annual plantings. Irwin's adviser on the planting was Jim Duggan. The garden manager is Richard Naranjo. Any negative reactions from the American landscape architecture profession become irrelevant when one watches visitors of every kind enjoying the variety of scent, color, and leaf in the garden.*

Irwin believes that every garden and landscape has a "power site." In this case, it is here, at the midpoint, when one turns away from the Los Angeles panorama and looks back over his garden embraced by the buildings of the Getty Center.

The treatment of the view from the slope led to another heated discussion with Meier. In his original plan for the garden, the grand staircase and terraces

These have a potential height of 120 feet. When they reach 60 feet, Irwin predicts that they will "read" in scale, improving the space vertically below and relating to Meier's buildings on each side of the garden above. Even now, they provide welcome cool shade after the blistering travertine stone setts of the arrival plaza. The French wicker café armchairs scattered around the plaza create an informal atmosphere and also serve as a design reference to the relaxed street life of France and *La Vie Douce*.

The simplest and yet perhaps the most effective element of Irwin's design is centered on the top tier of the amphitheater above the oval pool. Here the Cor-Ten steel walls retain gravel and provide a daring contrast to the arcs of the planting on either side. Angular crossovers are not only a design variation of the ramps across the serpentine stream, but they also provide the visitor with an enormous panorama of Los Angeles at a garden exit.

would have made his buildings completely open to the view. Irwin's solution is more exciting since it includes some elements of surprise, such as the plane trees of the water course. Irwin had the following words carved into a stone at the bottom of the serpentine water course, and they are an accurate reflection of the triumph of this garden:

Ever Present, Never Twice the Same
Ever Changing, Never Less Than Whole

**Above** *Contrast is another characteristic of Irwin's design game. Here a green lawn abuts Cor-Ten steel retaining walls. Sculptural clumps of grass rise out of the softer herbaceous and annual plantings.*

*The Therapeutic Garden demonstrates that human interaction with the landscape is a dynamic and vital experience that offers the promise of awareness, recovery, and transformation.*

Douglas Reed

## Therapeutic Garden for Children, Wellesley, Massachusetts
*Garden Honored with President's Award of Excellence, 1997 American Society of Landscape Architects*

Gardens have been perceived as places of sanctuary and healing for many thousands of years. This tradition is manifest in the healing gardens of hospitals and hospices today. Contemporary healing and therapeutic gardens are being designed and made to help AIDS patients, Alzheimer's and stroke sufferers, and many types of extreme psychological and traumatic disorders.

A sense of sanctuary is basic to the healing work of Douglas Reed's Therapeutic Garden for traumatized children near Boston. Reed was commissioned to design the garden by Dr. Sebastiano Santostefano, director of the Institute for Child and Adolescent Development, a treatment center for children suffering from the traumas of a variety of emotional and behavioral disorders. Santostefano and his therapists work on hidden trauma. Children who have witnessed illness, violence, or death are often his patients. He explains his approach by saying: "Early intervention is the basis of the institute's work. It operates in an elementary school in Boston, testing even the kindergarten children." Santostefano has definite views on restoring the mental health of children. They are never treated on the analyst's couch, or in the clinical and often oppressive conventional psychiatric facility. His success rate since 1993 has been excellent. It has been shown in subsequent studies that if testing and help can be given to children with traumas before the age of ten, then they will have three times less chance of developing behavioral or learning disorders in their teens.

For many years Santostefano had wanted to transform the rambling one-acre garden behind his large, three-story Victorian house. By creating a purpose-built garden, he hoped to combine

**Far right** *A young patient delights in the Therapeutic Garden for Children designed by Douglas Reed. Exploration of the garden, and the dialogue between therapist and patient that results, constitutes an important part of the treatment at the institute.*

### GARDEN STATISTICS

**Client:** Institute for Child and Adolescent Development

**Budget:** $250,000

**Designer:** Douglas Reed Landscape Architecture Inc.

**Area:** 1 acre

**Climate:** Zones 4–5

**Soil type:** Acidic loam

**Aspect:** Southeast

**Date of completion:** 1996

**Number of gardeners:** Contractor

his two main interests, therapy and nature, in one place. He wanted to make a garden where children of all ages could feel safe, and a place where even the most traumatized could begin to work out their problems.

Douglas Reed was eager to accept the commission. It was a challenge because it was the first garden of its type that his office had undertaken. He talked to Santostefano at length about the psychological implications of the landscape on therapy. They worked together to research the brief for the project by touring areas of natural beauty around Boston.

Reed described his role in the design process in the following words:

The director had long dreamed of developing a garden for use in therapy, and developed clear ideas about what the landscape should provide. My role as a landscape architect was to give form to those theories and ideas.

Mature stands of existing trees and a nine-foot change in elevation were the sources of inspiration for Reed's first drawings. In his own words, "The design expresses the narrative of a water course that weaves its way through the site, linking a sequence of spaces that correspond to the stages of a child's

recovery." The sunken area of the site was once the path of a stream. The knowledge that there had been water on the site led Reed to use it as the major design element. To him it symbolized life (as it has in gardens for millennia), and in this garden it also became a symbol of recovery.

The serpentine water course was inspired by the one at Rousham House in Oxfordshire, England. Rousham, one of the most admired and poetic of eighteenth-century English gardens, was designed in 1738 by William Kent. Reed's water course, the major unifying element of his design, is a low, eight-inch-wide steel-sided trough, partially filled with gravel. The water begins its journey on a stone terrace on one side of the institute. Reed thinks of the terrace and garden as a seamless extension of the building. The head of water rises first from a low, circular gray-green granite basin, spills gently over the edge, and flows out through five stainless-steel pipes in a wall. It then falls into a rill that the children follow through the garden. When the garden was judged for the American Society of Landscape Architects award, one of the judges commented: "I can just imagine a child putting something—a leaf, a stick, a sailboat—in this trough and watching it make its way through the landscape."

Reed envisaged his design as "a series of archetypal landforms carved by water." Following the rill as it falls from the terrace, children find a sequence of shapes. Some of them are extrovert shapes that rise

**Below** *The flowing lines of one of Reed's earliest sketches for the garden reflect the inspiration that Reed drew from his discovery that there had once been water on the site of the Therapeutic Garden.*

**Right** *The fluid contours revealed by a model of the garden dramatically illustrate Reed's attempt to create a landscape that seems to have been molded by the forces of water.*

up from the garden. There is a knoll, a mount, a bridge, an island, and an upland wood; others, such as the cave, the ravine, the shallow pond, and the glade, are obviously introvert. Reed wanted spaces to correspond to levels of recovery: a dark, narrow cavelike ravine conveys a sense of safety, an upland wooded area is for exploration, the steep and shallow slopes of the grassed-earth forms beg to be climbed, and a large, sunny glade suggests playing and running.

The different areas of the garden are defined by plantings of native species. In the upland section, among the existing red and white oaks, Reed planted Norway maple, and there are river birch with native gray and red osier dogwoods, common witch hazel, and arrowhead viburnum. The decorative shrubs include common box; Japanese, longstalk, and inkberry holly; mountain laurel; mock orange; lilac; and oakleaf hydrangea. The cave, for hiding and huddling in, is built from a shelter of transplanted Japanese yew. Liquidambar and pagoda dogwood, American beech, and woodland hydrangea are included with birches to furnish the ravine and ridge slopes. The island itself is actually a thicket of swamp azalea, clethra (summersweet), and amelanchier.

**Above** *The rill running through the garden was inspired by the water course at Rousham, the great eighteenth-century garden by William Kent in Oxfordshire, England.*

The pond is edged with fothergilla, ferns, yellow flag iris, and gooseneck loosestrife. At intervals along the lawn, drifts of blue squill have been set as a spring groundcover. In the lowland areas within the existing maple, pine, and cedar, Reed has planted more amelanchier, arrowhead viburnum, hay-scented fern, and lily-of-the-valley. The glade's existing black oak, yellow wood, and Canadian hemlock have been complemented with an understory of oakleaf hydrangeas, rosebay rhododendron, and *Viburnum mariesii*. The planting of various heights and the sequence of earth forms have meant that the garden is a continuing mystery for the children. It must be explored, for there is no one vantage point from which it can be viewed in its entirety.

The goal of the Therapeutic Garden is simple to outline but much more difficult to achieve. Among a variety of therapeutic techniques employed at the center, Santostefano now includes the exploration of the garden. The therapist and child establish a bond through the elements of the landscape. The behavior of a child at each of Reed's design incidents is documented by the therapist on a copy of the garden plan. Santostefano explains that "some memories are unlocked by sensation." He recalls the case of an adolescent girl's realization about her generalized anger while lying face-down on the mound in the garden. She told the therapist, somewhat hesitatingly, that she felt she was lying on the belly of a pregnant woman. Further discussion revealed that the girl's early trauma came from her mother having given birth to a stillborn child.

Santostefano's dream of a therapeutic garden was realized with the help of Judy Pillsbury, a Paris art dealer. Santostefano had treated a member of her family, and she spearheaded a drive to raise the first $200,000 needed to pay for the garden. The work of the institute goes beyond the boundaries of Douglas Reed's design, for the doctor is using the garden as a training ground for the paraprofessionals who will work on the institute's outreach program for adolescents in the socially and economically deprived South End area of Boston.

Reed thinks that the garden is one of the most satisfying he has ever designed. It is truly rewarding to see the tangible results among the children who have been treated there. The following passage, written by Mac Griswold, a leading American garden historian and writer, gives a marvelous insight into the purpose of the garden:

> Sanctuary has lost the power of repeated common ritual and shared community memory. Instead, what establishes a sacred public landscape in contemporary times is our often individual and nearly unconscious response to its peace and safety and beauty. Actions dictated by the design of the place itself, such as sitting, staring off between the trees, moving through space on a path, listening to the sound of water, or watching the slow patterns of shadow, are what restore power, hope, and psychological stability.

**Below** *The terrace with a low, green granite basin, the source of the rill that leads the children on a therapeutic journey of discovery through the garden.*

**Left** *The stone retaining wall of the terrace pierced by stainless steel pipes fed by the basin on the terrace above. A catchment pool then feeds the rill meandering through the garden.*

# Daniel Libeskind

## E. T. A. Hoffmann Garden, The Jewish Museum, Berlin

*I imagine that many people have read E. T. A. Hoffmann at some point. . . I have always loved E. T. A. Hoffmann, and I was stunned when I started working on the museum to discover that he was a lawyer in the Altbau, in the Kollegienhaus.*

Daniel Libeskind

| GARDEN STATISTICS |
| --- |
| **Client:** Berlin Senate |
| **Budget:** DM111.8 million (building and garden) |
| **Designer:** Daniel Libeskind |
| **Area:** 70 x 70 feet (garden) |
| **Climate:** North European |
| **Soil type:** Sand |
| **Aspect:** North |
| **Date of completion:** 1999 |

The Jewish Museum is adjacent to the Kollegienhaus, a baroque public building designed by Philipp Gerlach in 1725. E. T. A. Hoffmann worked there as a judge. The E. T. A. Hoffmann Garden was designed by Daniel Libeskind as an extension to the theme of the museum building. It is named after Ernst Theodore Wilhelm Hoffmann (1776–1822), the great nineteenth-century romantic writer.

Hoffmann is considered to have been Germany's most important storyteller. Even though he had prepared himself for a legal vocation. He was also a brilliant caricaturist, and this caused him trouble among the conventional bourgeois society of Posen as he caricatured local officials. The satiric drawings cost Hoffmann his job as government assessor, and he was exiled to the dull town of Plock. He continued to divide his time between drawing and music, and his first short literary work was published in 1803, *The Letter from a Monk to his friend in the City.* He continued to write while pursuing his legal work until his death in 1822.

There are three routes through the museum, which Libeskind prefers to call "roads." The first long one calls up the history of Berlin and its long continuity and leads to upper-floor exhibition galleries. Of the two others, the longer route goes to the dead-end "road of the Holocaust void" and the shorter to the memorial Garden of Exile and Emigration and two spaces of contemplation. The garden is Libeskind's metaphor, combining the image of so many Jews who left by sea and also a reference to the soil of Berlin. The memorial garden form is a hypostyle grid of forty-nine rough unclad concrete columns. The square of columns will eventually support a green roof.

In the top of each of the columns has been planted a willow-oak shrub (*Elaeagnus angustifolia*), and these are watered by an irrigation system that runs underground. These plants will grow together, forming a green canopy over the columns. The center column of the grid has been filled with earth gathered from Jerusalem and stands for Berlin; the other forty-eight contain earth from Berlin and symbolize 1948, when the state of Israel was formed. The hypostyle has been placed on the ground, which slopes in two directions, and all the columns tilt as a mass toward the museum. It is the only orthogonal right-angled square form to be found anywhere in the museum, the design being right-angled both in section and in plan. The garden

**Below** *The asymmetric pattern of stone setts in a variation on the pattern in the Paul Celan Courtyard.*

**Right** *An aerial view of the Hoffmann Garden adjacent to the Jewish Museum. The building's zigzag footprint is likened to the Nazi SS lightning insignia or a deconstructed Star of David.*

has a disturbing effect after experiencing the asymmetricality of the interior of the museum.

Libeskind's purpose was to disorient the visitor. It was to represent the "shipwreck of history." He wanted the visitor to feel unstable and even somewhat seasick. The garden and architecture of the building are to be experienced with both the head and the feet. Libeskind thinks architecture should first be experienced with the feet and then, later on, one can think about it. Libeskind has also called the garden of memorial the "upside-down" garden, a further metaphor referring to the displacement of Jews prior to World War II. Images for that experience are drawn from Libeskind's idea that Berlin looked very different to the exiles and even to Berliners who remained. The upside-down aspect of the garden emerges from the earth inside the concrete columns, the hard ground below, the roots at the top of the columns, and the willow-oak shrubs forming their canopy high above—inaccessible.

Other landscaping around the memorial garden consists of old species red and white roses planted in six-foot squares. The grid pattern is turned or skewed 15 degrees in relation to the museum, so "the roses dance with each other," according to Jan Wehberg, who consulted on the landscaping. The rose was chosen for its symbolic past associations: the thorny rose is a model for life in that it has the power to both injure and reconcile. The rose was also the only plant that was allowed in the ancient city of Jerusalem. Existing maple trees became part of the landscape design. A grove of spiny locust trees was planted as a contemporary inversion of the mythical motif of the Garden of Eden, the garden of paradise. The landscaping was designed by Cornelia Muller and Jan Wehberg, landscape architects who work in Berlin.

The garden was placed on an open side of the museum so that it engages the street life of the city. It also invokes other images. The route to the garden from underground is through a glass door that calls up the notion that freedom comes only through exile. The hypostyle grid of columns has associations with the urban grids of cities massed with skyscrapers, perhaps an image of haven for the Jews fleeing from Berlin.

Finally, there is a kind of garden in another courtyard of the museum. It is the Paul Celan Courtyard in honor of the Jewish poet, author of "The Death Fugue." Planted in the courtyard is Celan's favorite tree—a single paulownia.

E

**Far left** *A plan of the E. T. A. Hoffmann Garden of Exile and Emigration. The only orthogonal element in Libeskind's Jewish Museum design is the garden grid.*

F

**Below** *A transverse view of the Hoffmann Garden.* Elaeagnus angustifolia *grows from the tops of the columns, its horizontal growth will form a green roof over the hypostyle grid of columns.*

# Ton ter Linden

## Ruinen, Drenthe, Holland

*I see each border as a watercolor; light is all important. I like to use tall airy plants so you can see the light fall through them.*

Ton ter Linden

*Far right* Ton ter Linden's gloriously informal massed planting within his strict square and rectangular plan.

Impressionism and Pointillism: two definitions drawn from the history of painting could be used to describe this extraordinary garden in northeastern Holland. Ton ter Linden, the creator of the garden, is himself a fine painter. Early on, he experimented in oils but found them too thick and opaque for his flower and plant subjects. Watercolors became his preferred medium. They embodied the lightness and transparency that he expresses wonderfully in both his plant paintings and his gardens. Piet Mondrian, the great Dutch abstract artist of black-and-white grid paintings with blocks of color, also comes to mind when looking down at the strictly rectilinear plan of ter Linden's garden.

Ton ter Linden is a self-taught artist and garden designer. While growing up in Amsterdam, he loved the flowers his mother placed in the house. When he was older, he began making pencil sketches in the local parks, teaching himself about structure and line from the trees. Later he ventured into color and its myriad variations. It was in the Thysse Park in Amsterdam that he noticed the organic methods employed by the gardeners. Since then, he has never used pesticides or chemical fertilizers. Ton ter Linden bought his four-acre site in the rural province of Drenthe on a bleak, rainy day twenty years ago. It is an area of peaceful, open meadow land, with a scattering of small farms with thatched or grass-covered roofs. It was the perfect place to paint and garden.

For many years, ter Linden had dreamed of creating a garden. Here, land was cheap, and he could realize his ambition. His new home consisted of a small, rundown farm complete with disintegrating brick farmhouse, dilapidated barns, and neglected meadows. The only thing of beauty was a venerable apple tree, now over one hundred years old. Ton ter Linden used the tree as a lookout and as a vertical reference while he was in the process of designing the garden.

### GARDEN STATISTICS

**Designer:** Ton ter Linden
**Number of staff:** 2
**Area:** 4 acres
**Climate:** Northern temperate
**Soil type:** Peat
**Aspect:** South
**Date of completion:** Ongoing
**Number of gardeners:** 2

Hanne Cannegeiter, ter Linden's assistant, is very clear about the way plants are used in the garden: Ton's love of watercolors is apparent throughout his garden. There are no sharply defined areas of color next to one another, rather a moving interplay, one color drawn on by another. This style leads to a planting arrangement Ton calls "weaving," for which he may make use of so-called weaver-plants spread through a bed, simulating the effect of a mist in merging colours. For this purpose, some of his favorite plants are artemisia, nepeta, *Physostegia virginiana speciosa* 'Bouquet Rose.'

Gradation of height is the conventional Gertrude Jekyll legacy for the classic Arts and Crafts border, a historical norm flouted by ter Linden. He often plants tall, upright subjects at the front of a bed to give a sense of transparency and depth. He succeeds because of his vast knowledge of color, flowering times, and leaf and plant form. In autumn and winter, seed- and flowerheads add beauty to the foreground of a planting, rather than being massed in the background.

**Right** *Grasses in one of ter Linden's six "water borders." Ter Linden calculates the areas for the beds and positions his plants freehand, without the constraints of a paper plan.*

**Below** *The master plan of Ton ter Linden's garden not only recalls the grid paintings of his fellow countryman, the artist Piet Mondrian, but also echoes the super-precise agricultural field patterns of their homeland.*

THE GARDENS OF TON TER LINDEN

oenothera, solidago, and verbascum, creating his painterly plant composition. Roses are planted for contrast on the arbor and on eight-foot frames.

As one might expect, the Sun Border is in full sun. Conceived on a large scale, it is ninety-five feet long and twenty-one feet at its widest point. Here is the exception to ter Linden's "taller plants at the front" rule. Though mainly at the rear of the bed, they flow through its length in ribbons of color. Two of his favorite "big chaps," being both tall and luxuriant in growth, are *Veronicastrum virginicum album* and *Verbena hastata*. Both create a dramatic impact. He uses a broad color palette and contrasts plant shapes artfully.

The Yellow Garden is not the usual pale, almost monochromatic one to be found in other Dutch gardens or in some of the more prissy manor gardens in England. Ton ter Linden's vigorous artist-plantsman eye lays down a yellow core, then "weaves" in red, terracotta, and orange from plants selected to reach a climax in August. There are solid blocks of colour as he graduates tones of alchemilla, alstroemeria, helenium,

In autumn the dried seed- and flowerheads create a splendid visual effect. Leaving them uncut also has a practical purpose. It provides insulation for plants in the bed's understory, and according to the garden's guidebook:

It is forbidden to pick anything. In our way of gardening it is important that seeds are spread around the garden in a natural way.

Most of the taller plants need staking, and quantities of brushwood are used. In ter Linden's own words:

Birch is ideal because it is so pliable but I also use a lot of oak twigs. I start staking plants like delphinium and thalictrum when they are about two feet tall, but I also stake surrounding plants. In this way I create a network of brushwood which I hope will survive the inevitable gales. After staking I cut away all the superfluous wood, so nothing remains in sight.

Ter Linden waits until spring to work on his beds—the big clean-up. First, he removes and burns all of the spent brushwood. The dead stems of the herbaceous plants are then cut with shears into eight-inch lengths and spread over the bed. Here they become a layer of mulch fertilizer, aiding moisture retention during the summer. When this job is complete, ter Linden can embark on the weeding.

To vary the garden pictures for both adults and children, ter Linden has built a wooden platform that he calls the belvedere. It is only five feet high, but it offers the same perspective of the garden as that enjoyed by a low-flying bird.

Ton ter Linden's dislike of curves is played out in the herbaceous beds as well as the six "water borders." The leaves of plants and the arching stems of the grasses are mirrored by the surfaces of the pools. The garden changes, not only with the seasons but also with its owner's constant care and painterly eye.

**Above** *A mature climbing rose behind the serene pool on a summer evening. Its rounded, organic shape is an effective formal contrast to the geometric lines of the pool and benches.*

# Thomas Balsley

## Gantry Plaza State Park, Long Island City, Queens, New York

*What I hope drives the approach to Queen's West is sensitivity to the past.*

Thomas Balsley

Long Island City is the site of the Isamu Noguchi Garden Museum, where sculptures and a sculpture garden have been established for the work of Noguchi—one of the greatest influences on late twentieth-century landscape and garden design. We feel the shade of Noguchi must be smiling benignly down on this new two-acre waterfront plaza park, if for no other reason than the strong and sculptural use of stone that Balsley has employed in his design for the site.

*Far right  Local Long Island City residents are seemingly oblivious to the magical New York City skyline as they focus on the game in Thomas Balsley's Gantry Plaza State Park.*

The spectacular views from to the skyline of Manhattan was named for the huge black used to hoist railroad cars and for the westward journey, and they should not be swept and have become stunning some of the most imposing metropolis across the river. United Nations headquarters; view is of the Empire State Building, rising up within the

the park across the East River are a splendid bonus. The park steel gantries that were other cargo onto river barges Balsley was determined that away. They were cleaned up post-industrial frames for buildings of the electric One view is a "shot" of the a second and equally stunning Building and the Chrysler amazing skyscraper-scape of

that "wonderful town."

Queens West is part of a major redevelopment at the western end of Long Island. It is designed to be a combination of commercial and residential buildings over some seventy-three acres. The site, which is called Hunter's Point, covers a 114-mile linear waterfront strip on the edge of Long Island City. The total cost of the development is to be $2.3 billion. This will fund the construction of nineteen high-rise buildings, open spaces, and parks amounting to some twenty-five acres.

---

**GARDEN STATISTICS**

**Client:** Development Corporations: New York and New Jersey

**Budget:** $15 million

**Designers:** Thomas Balsley Associates

**Area:** 2 acres

**Climate:** Zones 4–5

**Soil types:** Clay and loam

**Aspect:** South and west

**Date of completion:** 1998 and ongoing

Local community alarm bells began to ring in the existing neighborhoods of Long Island City when the redevelopment project was initially announced. The inhabitants predicted that the proposed new buildings would be detrimental to their homes and would, at the very least, screen them from the waterfront and might well cut them off completely. All too predictably,

a stylish as well as an industrial quality.

Balsley has been commissioned to design three other public spaces within the Gantry Plaza project. The major works of North Gantry Park and South Gantry Plaza were completed in the spring of 1998. The Peninsula, which will span more than an acre, has yet to be installed.

**Below**  *Balsley designed robust split-faced granite blocks to retain the river bank and act as a park amenity.*

**Far right**  *The sculptural gantries were retained by Balsley as a historical reference to the railroad and river barge trade of the past.*

their suspicions were soon confirmed by the construction of a monolithic forty-two-story tower designed by Cesar Pelli. The height of this building alone confirmed the community's need for new open spaces and public parks. In response to the local outcry, Hunter's Point Community Park was built in 1996. It is situated on a relatively narrow patch of ground at the end of the main shopping street of Long Island City. Here Balsley was able to experiment with both hard and soft landscaping materials, which he would return to later in Gantry Plaza and the other parks. The stainless-steel "street furniture" with geometric patterns punched into it, the metal light fixtures, and the sail-shaped canopies combine to give the area both

North Gantry Park, to the south of the Peninsula, is the arrival and midpoint of the entire Gantry Plaza State Park design. It is best to arrive at the park on foot from Long Island City. Balsley has designed a circular fog fountain sitting in a small plaza, which is backed by a wall on which "Queens West" is written in large letters. The most immediately striking features here are the giant gantries. As Balsley says, "They create this moment that dominates your consciousness, but you have to think of them in context."

Lee Weintraub, who collaborated with Balsley on the project, agreed with his statement that the gantries represented a historical "take" and confirmed their use as sculptural design elements within the setting

**Right** *Lighting adds another dimension to the park. Plantings were designed to be rambling and slightly overgrown, producing a sense of the wildness of the site's indigenous plants when the river and railroad traffic ceased.*

EAST RIVER

**Above** *The master plan of Gantry Plaza State Park.*

of the park. As Weintraub said, "The gantries were always going to be a focus, or screen, through which to see the back wall of the space—the east side of Manhattan." They provide a strong vertical aspect to the design as well as a pleasing intermediate shape between the land and river, with its amazing panorama of skyscrapers.

The name of the locality, Long Island, is painted on the gantries in bold red-and-white-trimmed letters from the late nineteenth century. The developers' preference was for the name "Queens West," which appears in North Gantry Park. Balsley pushed for the use of the original name: "We wanted to build on the history of Long Island City as a center of manufacturing, a place where people actually made things."

The ground plane leading to the gantries has strong pairs of honed-stone paved stripes, which link and lead to pairs of rail tracks at the gantries. These are references to the time when the gantries' function was to heave up railroad cars onto river barges. The rail motif continues, leading the visitor out to the gantries and also to the four piers jutting out into the East River. Each pier has been designed with a different function, although they are all linked by the common elements of metal-pipe balustrading capped by rounded wooden railings. One pier is equipped with benches, and it

**Below** *Fishermen's bait, catch, and other equipment can all be left on this metal table. It is also equipped with stools and a faucet—a good setting for those discussions about "the one that got away."*

might eventually house a ferry terminal. The next has a raised metal counter like a bar and was described by Weintraub as "a place to sit down, put your elbows on a table, and eat lunch." The third pier looks more private, with its stylish, gently wavy, slatted wooden loungers. Finally, the fishing pier has a serpentine bench along its length, and at the end is a metal table designed for cleaning fish and bait in the purpose-built sink. It also has a tape measure fitted by one of the fishermen.

In all areas of the design Balsley has played with a wide range of materials: stone, gravel, metal, wood, and plants. The variations have come from his site-specific or site-generated approach to the design. The cut-stone arcs of steps and wall seats are inspired by the curves of the river bank. The hefty chunks of the split-faced granite steps are stacked at the water's edge, helping to retain the bank and bring visitors to its edge for Manhattan-viewing. To Balsley, the stone blocks suggest "the ruggedness of the railroad and reinforce the notion of the power of industry and its effect on this site." Gravel paths are sited among the asymmetrical planting beds, punctuated with more stone blocks and elegant wooden benches. The plantings have a purposely overgrown, unkempt, and slightly wild feeling, as though they were successors to the indigenous colonies of plants that grew up when the gantry, railroad, and barge operations stopped.

The interpretative area, which includes one of the gantries, was conceived as a "place to think about the past." Weintraub's view, which could be a controlling part of the inspiration, is that:

This area, including the gantry, was intended to suggest the way the place might have looked after the last rail car was loaded onto a barge, and the workers left—a kind of stabilized ruin.

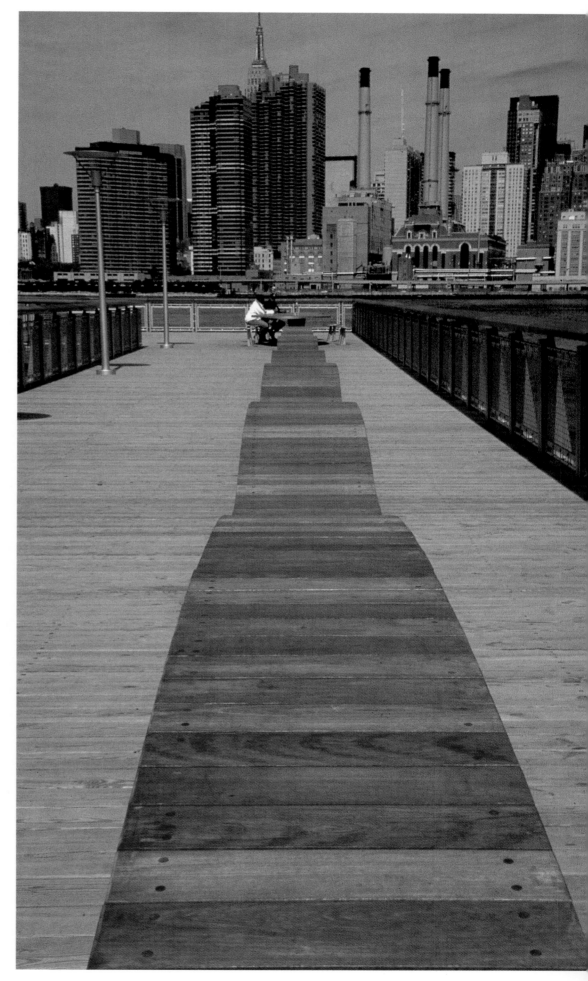

**Right** *A view of the wave-pattern wooden bench on one of the four river piers in the Balsley park design.*

*I pay no homage to the traditions of standard English-based picturesque garden-making. Where the landscape is deliberately man-made as in this situation, a designer doesn't have to relate to the natural context. I am driving this thing.*

Ted Smyth

# Ted Smyth

## Sanders Garden, Auckland, New Zealand

A native New Zealander and Aucklander, Ted Smyth has never traveled out of his native country, but his outlook could hardly be called "regional." His garden designs are extremely modernist and sophisticated. He says that he may have been influenced by the painting of Kandinsky and Modigliani, and by the music of Schoenberg, along with a "sighting" of the work of Noguchi. We wonder if he has secretly read *Topos* and *Domus*, the high-brow landscape and architecture journals, or even the occasional issue of the more middle-brow *Architectural Digest*.

**Far right** *The strong, sculptural shapes of the subtropical plants used by Smyth provide excellent foils for the white International Style house and pool.*

While growing up, Smyth was always interested in gardens. In high school he was fond of art and would bicycle for miles to sketch the landscape. He has always thought of himself as an artist. At one point he worked as a commercial artist. Later, to pay for time to paint, he became a manual worker. Ted Smyth is a self-taught garden designer who has created his own distinct language of design. As he says: I have always ignored the traditions. I prefer to define space structurally, sometimes with planting, sometimes with hard materials. I enjoy setting up volumes of space. An architect sets volumes of space as a mass; sometimes I like to set it up in reverse.

He has been influenced very little by the major strands of contemporary garden design. Having always thought of himself as an artist, he only began to design gardens because he had to pay the bills. This compelled him to redirect his considerable, and now brilliantly realized, creative energies to the landscape. Smyth recalls his early days as a designer of gardens somewhat wryly:

**GARDEN STATISTICS**

**Client:** Darrin and Leslie Sanders

**Budget:** NZ $650,000

**Designer:** Ted Smyth

**Area:** 21,388 square feet

**Climate:** Temperate subtropical

**Soil type:** Varies (all imported)

**Aspect:** North

**Date of completion:** 1996

**Number of gardeners:** 3

I used to have nightmares about making landscaping into art. There was the problem of fitting in the lifestyle commodities, which are the antithesis of art! It was important for me to keep believing I was an artist.

Two other artists of influence on contemporary landscape design in the twentieth century, Luis Barragán and Isamu Noguchi, also redirected their creative energies from architecture and sculpture to garden and landscape design. They would be considered self-taught too.

Smyth is now becoming, quite correctly, internationally recognized as a garden designer. We first saw his work in the *Harvard Design Magazine* in 1997. The article featured the Sanders Garden in Auckland, the subject of this case study. The house is a white, modernist, angular, glass-and-stucco design built in the 1980s. It was designed by Rolly Adams of the Auckland practice of Adams Langley.

Smyth was first asked to revamp the entry courtyard. Then he was commissioned to rework the entire garden, an empty rectangle with two trees. He was made designer and overall project manager for the year of garden installation.

In the rectangular garden space, Smyth has played with the design, echoing the curves, ellipses, and rectangles in the architecture of the house. The patterns and shapes are repeated in the paving, the swimming pool, and the perimeter walls—constructed of both plaster and metal. Achieving a harmony between the house and the design of the garden was a particular concern of Smyth's:

The integration of the house and the garden with the architecture is very important, important with this particular house because it is so very strong. But it's important with virtually every garden. Landscape architects/designers shouldn't decide to use structure in a garden and willfully ignore the architecture of the building. But many do. Generally, landscape architects/designers in New Zealand haven't yet learned to integrate their work with architecture either overtly or poetically.

Smyth has used a typically restrained range of materials: stainless steel, stone, marble, water, and sculptural plants. He defines his attitude to the materials of hard landscaping in the following words:

I like the anonymity and modernity of materials. They shouldn't be too animated like terra cotta, brass, or gold, which are like busy, noisy animals. They interfere too much. In order to create serenity and spatial quality you have to reduce the personality of the materials. Even the plants, although they are sculptural and striking, have to work with the other elements.

The swimming pool area is the largest design element in the garden. It is extremely attractive, for it is a generous enough size for a good swim. Smyth's detailing has made the pool visually exciting. It is minimal-modernist-ornamental hybrid. Instead of the conventional rectangular or kidney-shaped pool, Smyth has used zigzag or stepped corners, a pattern repeated on the profile of a plastered boundary wall. A quiet

**Below** *A side view of the Sanders house and garden, for which Smyth created the landscape elements.*

**Left and above** At night the pool area is transformed into a mysterious sculptural landscape. Trees that during the day take second place to hard landscaping elements are dramatically uplit, and the distinction between horizontal and vertical is blurred by reflections in the pool.

**Above** *The lush greenery of cycads and other subtropical plantings around the driveway of the Sanders house perfectly complements the cool white lines of the angular modern house.*

inlet on one side of the pool has a row of water jets eighteen inches above the water level. Four low, elegant steps create waterfalls beneath a dramatic, tubular stainless-steel sculpture on axis with the center of the house.

The design stroke within the sculpture is a beautiful graceful band, or arc, of thin stainless-steel elements, contrasting with the strong uprights of the stainless-steel tubes. The sculpture highlights another of Smyth's heartfelt beliefs:

> One of my philosophies is that you have to take a risk, rather than sitting in a predictably safe seat. You have to be prepared to put your money where your mouth is. That sculpture, for instance, it could have been an absolute disaster. When you have created something on that scale, you just can't take it down again.

Backing the sculpture and running behind the pool is another splendid perimeter fence, a louvered screen of thin, stainless-steel pieces set as horizontal bands.

Textural contrasts abound: the stainless steel is a sleek counterpoint to the pool, white plaster, and the dramatic sculptural planting:

> Paring back colors to almost black and white means that what you see is what you get. You can't rely on bright colours to hang it together. If your forms are wrong, you can't rely on the planting to disguise it. There are no crutches or wheelchairs here.

Other landscape designers in New Zealand credit Smyth with having broadened the selection of native and foreign subtropical plants available there. He likes

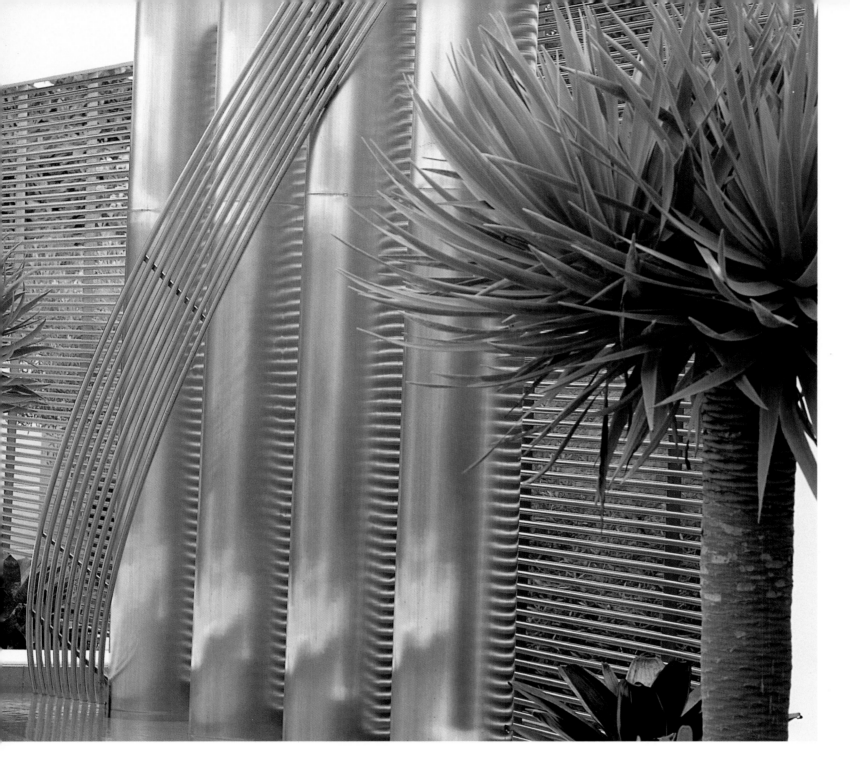

to use plants such as *Dracaena draco*, *Aloe bainesii*, and *Cycas revoluta*—specimens that are more likely to be found in select botanic gardens in northern temperate climates.

Like all the best landscape designers, Smyth places the planting plan himself, but he is the first to admit that he didn't always get it right:

> I like structural plants. I planted *Dracaena draco* when no one else knew about them. *Aloe bainesii*, *A. thraskii*, and *A. plicatilis* all have this structural look. And I like strap-leaved plants—clivia are good flowers for the shade. So are scadoxus with their big leaves. I scout around and go to specialist growers. Initially I did some horrific planting, I used to use shrubs—now I don't like them as well . . . It's important to keep moving on and developing so people can't imitate me, I'm devious in the nicest possible way.

The imaginative use of plants is not an element of Smyth's work that would immediately spring to the minds of many commentators when considering Smyth's gardens. In his own words:

> It has been said about my work that I sacrifice nature on the altar of the contemporary, but I prefer to say that I distill the essence of the spirit of nature.

**Above** *Ted Smyth's stainless-steel wall sculpture behind the pool of the Sanders house is a bold masterstroke that demonstrates Smyth's willingness to take risks with a design.*

# Desvigne & Dalnoky

## Urban Park, Issoudun, France

*We have no wish to imitate nature. We are fascinated by . . . sites whose constant and dramatic restructuring cannot be mapped: lagoons, deltas, dunes, river banks, ravines. It is incredible . . . that there should be a wide gulf between knowledge of nature and the inexplicable survival of picturesque garden stereotypes.*

Michel Desvigne and Christine Dalnoky

Desvigne and Dalnoky were trained at the Ecole Nationale Supérieure du Paysage at Versailles. Since it was founded in 1973, the college has been credited with being a major influence on the new approach to French landscape design. Students are taught that the design should be based on the features of the existing landscape and should not be seen merely as decoration.

Michel Corajoud and Alexandre Chemetoff, professional landscape architects, theorists, and teachers, devised the syllabus to be a combination of "academic" training in the techniques and theories of landscape architecture and of practical experience. Chemetoff designed some of the plantings for the Parc de la Villette, the former nineteenth-century slaughterhouse and cattle market, reworked as a public park in the north of Paris.

The college's approach can be summed up in these four basic tenets: anamnesis, preparation, in-depth vision, and relative thinking. Anamnesis is the analysis of the layers of signs that a site holds. It is the review of all that has happened there to shape it into a specific landscape. Preparation sees and evaluates the site as process, in the context of all the natural elements of its topology: the cycle of seasons, the climate, the recycling of water, the alternations of day and night, of growth and decline. In-depth vision "reads" a site in all its layers and complexities as a habitat, rather than as an open space to be filled with decorative, historical pattern-book designs. Relative thinking involves the site and the setting beyond its boundaries. This relates to the examination of the relationship between buildings and other, peripheral spaces such as roadsides and the uncultivated areas of "non-places." The important contemporary views of the Ecole du Paysage on process in garden and landscape design

| GARDEN STATISTICS | |
|---|---|
| **Client:** | City of Issoudun |
| **Budget:** | FF4 million |
| **Designers:** | Desvigne & Dalnoky |
| **Area:** | 7½ acres |
| **Climate:** | North European |
| **Soil type:** | Neutral |
| **Aspect:** | Full sun |
| **Date of completion:** | 1994 |
| **Number of gardeners:** | 2–5 |

**Below** *The designers have "substituted" a public park for an existing group of municipal vegetable plots. Substitution is an important part of their theory and practice.*

**Right** *Blossoming fruit trees edge the boardwalks that surround the new lines of planting. Some of the trees were already there, and some are newly planted. Together they create a reference to medieval strip planting.*

are echoed internationally in the work of landscape architects and designers such as Robert Irwin, creator of the Lower Central Garden at the Getty Center in Los Angeles; George Hargreaves, chairman of Landscape Architecture at Harvard; West 8 and Adriaan Geuze in Holland; and Torres and Lapeña in Spain.

Desvigne & Dalnoky, based in Paris, works mainly in France. It has also completed projects in both Italy and Spain and is now designing the Greenwich Reach landscape in London for the Millennium Experience in the year 2000. There is also a major unbuilt plan in former East Berlin involving the contemporary reworking of the Lustgarten Platz. A great 350-room palace in the Versailles style here was destroyed during World War II.

The design for this uncharacteristically large site demonstrates the historical awareness, meticulous analysis, and simplicity inherent in all of the designs of Desvigne & Dalnoky. Trees on grid plans would cover the entire square as an echo of the dense treescapes in Berlin. In the center of the square the firm proposed a large stone stepped and raised square called the Monument Garden, the site of a group of flowering trees that would be called the Sacred Grove. The square is designed to reflect the grandeur and historical importance of the former palace, and the existing grandeur of the Berlin Cathedral and the Altes Museum, which are nearby. Desvigne & Dalnoky has proposed a very few key design elements to be utilized with their characteristic elegant simplicity.

The Urban Park is much smaller in scale and is situated on the edge of a provincial town. The site is part of the town of Issoudun in the Indre region on the northern edge of the Massif Centrale. The 7½-acre

**Left** *Walking along the River Theol or fishing there has become much easier since the boardwalks were built.*

riverside site is the French version of the British muncipal vegetable plot. Small gardens and orchards have been tended there for generations. The objective was to create a small urban park on a very limited budget, using a design that not only recognized the history of the patch but was inspired by it.

Desvigne and Dalnoky have used one of their basic design tenets: to vary the familiar aspects of site content with elements of substitution making the new design. They exploded the original scale of the small "allotment" plots into a grid of four large squares, subdivided into four smaller ones. The formality of their skewed, contemporary grid is an expression of the *regulier* style intrinsic to the landscape heritage of France. Think of the four-square grid patterns (both macro and micro) to be seen endlessly in any of the great seventeenth-century French gardens by André Le Nôtre. Another reference to that formal style is the grouping of trees planted in allées, some complete and some irregular.

The center of the grid is on axis with the historic buildings in the main part of the town across the river: a medieval bell tower—La Tour Blanche—a church, a bridge, bastions, and museums. Two halves of the grid are bounded by rough wooden boardwalks, and the corner of one is cantilevered out over the River Theol. The boardwalks are practical for winter walks, for the ground near the river can become soft during that season. The wooden

planks have weathered down to a recessive gray color. Irises have been planted in long rows, making a pretty display in the early spring.

This part of the design and the straight lines of trees and shrubs in other parts of the grid carry a reference to an earlier time in European history, to the medieval system of strip farming. Here at Issoudun, lines of tall willow trees have been planted close to the houses lying adjacent to the park. In the next section of the grid there are straight lines of shrubs of medium height, and beyond is the grid of iris beds. Desvigne and Dalnoky's design is unique, for they have been inspired to make gentle but elegant design references to both their country's history of peasant agriculture and, using the four-square grid, to the refined apogee of garden design at the court of Louis XIV.

**Below** *Plan of the Urban Park, Issoudun. The plan of the park emerged from axis lines to main landmarks in the town across the river.*

# Rios Associates

## Satellite Courtyard, Long Beach, California

*There's often a fear that goes along with technology, but when you enter this space, you're not afraid of these dishes; you feel connected to them, and realize they are beautiful forms. Technology can be very beautiful.*

Mark Rios

In all cultures and over many millennia, humans have used whatever technology and building materials were available to make structures that reach up toward the sky. The pyramids of Egypt, southern India, and Mexico; the spires of the great medieval cathedrals of western Europe; and the "fingers reaching up to God" of the slender, wooden spires of New England churches—all represent the human yearning to reach upward, toward the unknown.

Stonehenge on England's Salisbury Plain and the many stone circles in Ireland, Scotland, and Brittany are other examples of humanity trying to communicate with the heavens. So too are the huge snake and water-spider mounds made by the Amerindians of the Missouri River basin and the giant animal shapes drawn out in stone lines by the Indians of the Nazca plain in Peru.

Computer-linked communications satellites, the godlike technological toys of human-kind, now spin through the less obviously spiritual skies of the late twentieth century, giving us the capacity to communicate instantly world-wide. Instead of stone, earth, and wood, we see power pylons, radio towers, and satellite dishes of metal as the vertical "marks" on the contemporary landscape.

Mark Rios, a landscape architect with a practice based in Los Angeles, has transformed a former parking lot in Long Beach, California, into a sculptural landscape. In the subject of this case study, he has used the high-tech signal-receiving antennae satellite dishes as the central design element of the Satellite Courtyard. Rios's client can be located at 118°11'west longitude and 33°46'north latitude. These are the map coordinates that locate Hughes Communications Inc., a major supplier of high-tech satellite-dish receiving antennae.

*Far right* *"Saucer pots" are a witty, practical variation on the high-tech dishes in the Satellite Courtyard. The pots are planted with dwarf forms of white-flowered plumbago, Australian bluebell creeper, and evergreen star jasmine.*

## GARDEN STATISTICS

**Client:** Hughes Communications Corporation Inc.

**Budget:** N/A

**Designer:** Rios Associates

**Area:** 1½ acres

**Climate:** Sunny and dry

**Soil type:** Sandy

**Aspect:** West

**Date of completion:** 1996

**Number of gardeners:** 2–3

Many late-twentieth-century, high-tech industries with main headquarters in the silicon valleys near San Francisco have outposts in the southern part of the state.

The Satellite Courtyard has been placed at the front of the company's building to mark it for new visitors and potential clients. It also serves as a place for employees to sit and take a break. The satellite dishes here bring to mind the three-dimensional or bas-relief signs that used to hang from shop fronts: the three golden balls of a pawn shop, the cigar-store Indian, or even the painted barbershop pole used in nineteenth-century America. Mark Rios has updated this traditional artisan concept to create a high-profile corporate identity in front of Hughes Communications' headquarters.

The Satellite Courtyard is the starting point for a tour of the Hughes Building. Visitors and new clients are stunned to learn that the satellite dishes are not just obsolescent hardware but antennae taking signals from satellites out in space. These signals are converted

into video images for the home television screens of America, controlled by the television networks that are Hughes Communications' principal clients.

The notion of using the satellite dishes as landmarks to signpost the Hughes headquarters originally came from architect Andrea Cohen Gehring, the design director at Widom Wein Cohen in Los Angeles. The satellites in the courtyard provide the opening beat to the two-story rotunda in the center of the building. Here models of satellites are displayed in front of a trompe l'oeil painting of outer space.

Generally, architects ask landscape designers to "shrub up" the area around their buildings, although some tend to think of the planting around their "amazing" structures as "green slime." Gehring was looking for something more elaborate, and Rios Associates was called in to implement the broad concept.

Rios began by investigating not only the subject of satellite dishes but also material from ancient civilizations, such as the artifacts associated with humanity's

**Above** *An aerial view of the Satellite Courtyard, showing the communication dishes set in a robust grid of stone and gravel.*

**Below** *A plan of the Satellite Courtyard.*

**Above** *Cutout concrete plinths are provided for employees to enjoy lunch or a break; shade is given by crape myrtle, coral, and snow gum trees pruned to fifteen feet so they do not block the satellite dishes.*

attempts to commune with its gods. The prehistoric, circular, monolithic shapes and the conformation of the satellite shape itself triggered the design ideas that became the Satellite Courtyard.

The dishes were perceived by Rios and his project designer, Corinne Capiaux, as beautiful, sculptural objects. Each of the twelve dishes measures ten to seventeen feet in diameter. They were placed on square concrete plinths, eighteen inches high. These were set out on a three-by-four grid, bounded by a high black chain-link fence. Black was chosen to make the fence recede into the background. It also made the white satellite dishes more striking. A circular fourteen-foot-high silver stainless-steel mesh fence, with a diameter of ninety feet, surrounds the entire site, providing maximum security. The plan of the design is a square in a circle, the reverse of that other endlessly pleasing and ancient pairing: the circle in the square (the magnificent floor in the Pantheon, Rome, being the most perfect example from antiquity).

In an area between the two fences, Rios has placed other concrete plinths of varying cutout shapes to encourage different-sized groups of people to sit there. These seating plinths continue the central grid pattern of the satellite bases. Rios thinks of them as

huge, raised-up blankets that you can lie down on or spread out a picnic lunch on, or, you can sit with your feet in the holes in the middle, almost like sitting at a Japanese table.

The planting near other buildings in the area is fairly business-park-standard. There are tall trees, grass-covered earth mounds, and an underplanting of shrubs. Rios wanted the Satellite Courtyard to be a complete contrast to its surroundings. He wanted to create something very minimal and Zenlike, so visitors would feel that they had arrived at a special place.

The company is pleased with the Satellite Court-yard. It is a dramatic signal of their location and products, and a relaxing area for employees, and having the satellites nearby has proved cost effective.

# Charles Jencks

*Nature is basically curved, warped, undulating, jagged, zigzagged, and sometimes beautifully crinkly. It never looks like a Platonic temple.*

Charles Jencks

## The DNA and Physics Garden of the Garden of Cosmic Speculation, Borders area, Scotlan

**Far right** *DNA sculpture of the sense of taste, the giant mouth suspended above two species of wild strawberry, in the DNA and Physics Garden.*

Is this extraordinary twentieth-century landscape a return to the design philosophy of William Kent and his belief that "nature abhors a straight line"? Charles Jencks is the leading thinker and guru of postmodernism. In 1990, Jencks and his late wife Maggie Keswick, an authority on Chinese gardens, began to create a stupendous and influential late-twentieth-century landscape. It consists of several gardens of varying sizes on forty acres of an estate among the low, rolling hills of southern Scotland. chaos and complexity theory combined with feng shui, ancient Chinese geomancy, are the two philosophical strands of thinking, practice, and inspiration. These elements were combined with the skills of master craftsmen: a mason, a carpenter, and metalworkers. There have also been many close encounters with massive diggers and earth-moving equipment. Charles Jencks continues to alter, add to, and improve this extraordinary concept.

Chinese geomancy is derived from the Taoist tradition of seeing what monks and philosophers following the great teacher Lao-Tzu called the "bones of the earth" in its waters, valleys, hills, and mountains. All these features contain the currents of invisible energy, *ch'i*, the vital spirit of earth, the cosmic breath of subterranean dragons. Today, Hong Kong businessmen bring in the geomancer to divine where their postmodern skyscrapers should be built. With high land values and limited space, today's geomancer has little choice but to get it right the first time. Jencks, a qualified architect and teacher, documented the postmodern in contemporary architecture. He continues to identify new trends, some of which are set out in his book *The Architecture of the Jumping Universe*. The book includes a straightforward exposition of the philosophy behind these gardens:

**Right** *In consultation with Charles Jencks, Liane Wilcher made this superb symbolic, axonometric, computer-generated drawing from the scanned photographic images that she took in the DNA and Physics Garden.*

**Far right** *Double-helix sculptures of the five senses (top to bottom): touch, hearing, taste, sight, and smell.*

**Right** *An overview of the DNA and Physics Garden, Jencks's visionary, complex, unique, and witty contemporary adaptation of the traditional vegetable patch.*

Our first assumption was that nature's forms are continuously changing and curved, as we applied this notion to drawing together the hills, streams, hedges and walls. During this time I was researching developments in recent science and cosmology—what is called "non-linear dynamics," or, more popularly, Chaos Theory. I was working on [*Architecture in a Jumping Universe*] which argues that design must look to science and contemporary cosmology if it is to recapture the depth and conviction it had in previous eras. Furthermore, these disciplines are telling us something surprising, positive.

The universe, it now appears, is much more creative, self-organizing and unpredictable than anyone had thought 20 years ago, when it was most commonly thought of as a complex machine. Contrary to the Newtonian view of scientific determinism and the Christian view of Genesis, the universe is, in fact, cosmogenic, meaning that it jumps all of the time to new levels of organization. . . . The new sciences of Complexity, of which Chaos is just one of 20, show the omnipresence of these sudden leaps at all scales.

Jencks's "jump" here is an enormous one within the context of contemporary landscape architecture and design. Frank Gehry has this to say about Jencks's cosmogenesis theories:

> Charles is the only architectural writer I know who will go way out on a limb, saw the limb off, fall through the air, grab another limb, and start all over again. That's what I love about him. He's willing to stick his neck out.

Jencks says that the starting point for the Garden of Cosmic Speculation was the dining room of his house. He and Keswick called it the Dragon Dance Room, for it is used for Scottish reels as well as cooking and dining. The decoration there is nonlinear; patterns and shapes are emphasized with curving folds and waves.

The axis of the gardens begins below the house and moves down the slope. Jencks has given them witty and wonderful names. First comes the Dry Cascade and the Maze Brain. The Garden of Fair Play is the tennis court; beyond it is the DNA and Physics Garden; and finally appears the largest and most dramatic incident: the fifty-foot spiral mound. Jencks says that this has several names, all denoting a similar shape—snail, ziggurat, mound. It is bounded by two different spirals, which only meet at the top. As they ascend, the paths rise and fall. As a result, in order to go up the mound, you sometimes have to go down, and vice versa. Nearby is the four-hundred-foot-long double-wave earthwork, which is called the snake or S-shaped earthwork.

These earthworks and the similar pair of lakes in which the exquisite grassed spiral—or paisley shape— is sited are the largest parts of this grand design. The

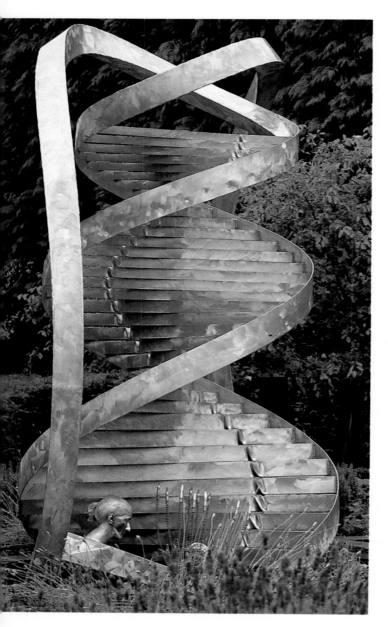

**Above** *A woman with her brain exposed symbolizes female intuition. She is sitting beside a double-helix sculpture. This is Jencks's design for the sixth sense: anticipation.*

grass mound and double-wave require one gardener cutting full-time April to September to mow them, supervised by the head gardener, Alistair Clark.

It is the DNA and Physics Garden that is the focus of this case study. The formal beds are planted in waving lines that follow the curves and lines of the unfolding DNA. This linear pattern of waves underlies the whole garden, and in this area it is miniaturized and planted with vegetables, flowers, fruit, and healing herbs, just as would have been in the traditional *physick* garden of a monastery or manor house. Local red sandstone rubble makes the Dragon Walls, a pair of superb, gently hump-backed enclosures. In one there are three openings to view the DNA and Physics Garden. (The stone grilles covering these openings are reminiscent of similar features in the traditional gardens of Soochow, China.) Through the grilles the circle for Edible Harmony, the square for Physical Reason, and the triangle for Kitchen Justice are visible. These witty wordplays are carved under each of the openings. All of the stonework is by a local master mason, Hugh Drysdale.

The DNA and Physics Garden is altered and improved annually by Jencks, but the basic grid plan of its formal parterre is constant and based on the five human senses plus the sixth sense, the female sense of intuition or anticipation. Each area is centered around a sculptural version of the DNA double helix. *Sight* is perhaps the most dramatic of these. It contains a miniature version of the fifty-foot-high spiral mound in the shape of a double helix. Inside the mound is a grottolike room, with crinkly black and white

fractal-banded wall patterns. At the top is an opening in the shape of an M. On bright days this casts the form of the letter inside the room, as a commemoration of Jencks's late wife, Maggie. *Smell* is represented by fragrant thyme plants that encircle the flared nostrils of a nose from which Jencks wants the smell of rotten vegetables to exude. *Hearing* is an ear trumpet finial that pivots in the wind activating chimes and bells. *Touch* is a sculpted hand rising above thistles and nettles, enclosed by a DNA double helix built of blocks. *Taste* has an aluminum mouth and thyme suspended above two species of wild strawberry. Finally, *Anticipation* is a woman looking at her open brain as it receives impulses from her fingers, which wave in the breeze—the sense of intuiting the future by picking up and interpreting vibrations.

Jencks's three-dimensional realizations of historical and current concepts of the universe are playful and wacky but also visionary, brilliant, and extremely serious. The stone gate piers at entrances to the DNA

We think of the DNA and Physics Garden as the "micro" versions of the theories played out by Jencks in the "macro" shapes of the grassed mound and the double-wave earthworks. The miniature grassed mound with its grotto is the best example.

The Garden of Cosmic Speculation is not only a grand, amusing, and serious creation, but also engages an audience from all backgrounds. An expert on Tudor gardens "read" the mound as a medieval castle lookout. An expert on eighteenth-century gardens was reminded of the enormous, grassed verges of the Moon Ponds at Studley Royal in Yorkshire. The sculpted grass theater at Claremont in Surrey also comes to mind, as does Hogarth's Line of Beauty. To others, it evokes images of land art in the United States in the 1960s and prehistoric earthworks in other parts of the world. The range of these reactions shows the power of the garden's rhythm and beauty as a visionary landscape, theories of the universe notwithstanding.

and Physics Garden put a contemporary "spin" on the traditional pineapple or eagle finials of the seventeenth and eighteenth centuries: on the left, the old view of the universe in bronze; on the right, the new in aluminum. These unique metal spheres represent a model of the major theories propounded about the universe: Ptolemaic, constellational, armillary, atomic, the Gaia hypothesis, and the universe as a whole.

*Left* Jencks's galactic seat of seven galactic spirals. It is cast concrete, and the lead finish is from blue-gray paint.

*Below and below left* The sense of sight: a micro spiral "eye" mount in the DNA and Physics Garden is a miniaturized version of the double spiral mount in the larger, cosmological landscape nearby. The fantastic interior of the eye mount features the oculus surmounting a metamorphosis of black optically vibrating waves.

# Jacques Wirtz

## Parterre du Carrousel, Tuileries, Grand Louvre, Paris, France

*The drawings of other designers often surprise me. Such good graphics, but they seem to work without knowing about plants. I cannot really believe in a designer who does not live in a garden.*

Jacques Wirtz

**Far right** *An aerial view of a single, raised parterre of yew hedges and linden trees. Its twin is across the Grand Louvre courtyard; both frame the Arc du Carrousel, the center of the design by Wirtz International.*

Inexorably, time and history move on, bringing change and destruction to our landscapes and gardens, which are some of the most ephemeral products of civilization. In France, three hundred years of garden history separate two major re-creations of the formal gardens of the Tuileries in Paris.

The existing Tuileries gardens were first created for Catherine de Medici in the sixteenth century. Since the early seventeenth century, they have been open to the public. André Le Nôtre (1613–1698) was in the third generation of the family of head gardeners to the French royal household, and he grew up in the Tuileries. In 1664 he was given the job of transforming the site. His new design included the main stone terraces adjacent to the Place du Carrousel.

In France, the current arts establishment threw up their hands in *horreur* when a Belgian landscape design practice was commissioned to redesign part of the Tuileries. Wirtz International, headed by Jacques Wirtz and his two sons, Peter and Martin, won the competition for the redesign of the Parterre du Carrousel on the east side of the gardens. The French call the reworking and restoration of historical gardens a continuation. The Wirtz design is but another layer in the long history of the gardens. In the past, Wirtz's work has been described by one critic as "a modern reflection on well-known tradition . . . uniting in his gardens as much beauty of the past as visionary force of the future." The design for the Place du Carrousel confirms this. The Arc du Carrousel dates from Napoleonic times. It is set on the grand axial vista of Paris that starts from the glass pyramid by I. M. Pei in the Louvre courtyard, goes through the centre of the Tuileries and up the Avenue de Champs-Elysées, and finally centers on the Arc de Triomphe and the Grande Arche de la Défense. This

### GARDEN STATISTICS

**Client:** Etablissement du Grand Louvre

**Budget:** FF65 million

**Designer:** Wirtz International

**Area:** 10¾ acres

**Climate:** Temperate

**Soil type:** Sandy loam

**Aspect:** West

**Date of completion:** 2001

**Number of gardeners:** 6

is the western end of the arc of *grands projets* for Paris, commanded by François Mitterrand. On the eastern point of the arc is the new opera house in the Bastille and the large public Parc de la Villette.

Some commentators say that the Mitterrand government was able to get away with the contemporary designers' competition for the new Tuileries gardens because the works were within the package of national garden restoration. This included the twenty-year renovation of the gardens at Versailles—the model of the formal garden style of Louis XIV, interpreted, clarified, and codified by Le Nôtre. In creating their design, the Wirtz team had to honor France's tradition of formal design while also acknowledging the contemporary.

Wirtz refers to the classical influence on his work as "the wisdom of our ancestors." His son Peter attributes much to their nationality:

> Belgium has always been strongly influenced by French gardens with their formality (and England with its loose romantic tradition), and by Germany, too; it's the same in music, art, and cuisine. We're a country where the cultures come together. In garden design here, there is a great mix, and many styles exist side by side.

Wirtz's design for the Grand Louvre project is centered on the Arc du Carrousel. Peter Wirtz gave the following explanation of the intention of their design:

> We wanted not only to create a buffer but part of a green world between the hard glass and stone surfaces of Mr. Pei's pyramid of glass and the Louvre courtyard, and make the Arc du Carrousel a true gate. It formerly seemed too small in that desert of stone. Now, it's like a keyhole to the rest of the gardens. Go through it and you find radials—rows of clipped yew hedges like projecting fingers.

The radial hedges recall the box hedges in the Wirtz's private garden in Schoten. They edge the paths of the former kitchen garden of the nearby château. They have lost their knife-edge geometry and changed into low, organic billows of green. Over the past forty-five years, the hedge has become a Wirtz trademark:

> I use it as a readable element, to provide equilibrium. I gained a certain reputation and indeed made à la mode—a term I detest—the use of box. But not in the style of Le Nôtre, in my own style.

Framing the Place du Carrousel and its arch is a pair of raised parterres in the classical, formal language of geometric shapes. Squares, rectangles, a circle, and an oval lead up to the middle of each parterre, and in the center is a clipped, square palisade of linden tree canopies on clear trunks. Within the hedge patterns and the linden tree squares, and asymmetrically placed among the radial yew hedges, is the national collection of eighteen bronze statues by Aristide Maillol. They were given to the country by Dina Vierny—the artist's

**Above** *Stone paving lines diverge from the Arc du Carrousel and then connect to radiating yew hedges, making visual and physical links to the redesigned Tuileries gardens.*

**Right** *Half of the large plan by Wirtz International.*

**Right** *The national collection of sculptures by Aristide Maillol is arranged among the yew hedges radiating from the center point of the Arc du Carrousel and on raised parterres to the right of the arch and behind it on the left.*

model. André Malraux, then minister of culture, had them placed here in 1964 to create a sculpture garden.

Jacques Wirtz balks at labels, preferring not to talk about a particular garden style. To him, trying to explain a garden is a kind of betrayal: "A garden is like a painting or piece of music; it should speak for itself."

The installation of the Tuileries garden was not an easy project. The historic significance of the site combined with the Wirtz practice's foreign nationality and high levels of bureaucracy meant that each and every trip to Paris was *une grande bataille* to realize the approved design. Contemporary innovation in Wirtz's classical designs will reach another high point when the fire, water, and air (artificial fog) elements are installed to celebrate the millennium at Alnwick Castle in England for the Duchess of Northumberland.

"I would be a very bad professor at a school of horticulture," says Wirtz. "Once an interviewer . . . asked me about my theory of design. I said, 'Give me a plan and I'll make you a garden. But don't ask me about theories.' "

# Jack Lenor Larsen

### LongHouse Garden,
### East Hampton, Long Island, New York

*Gardening appeals to us all the more when we are caught up in the whirlwind beyond ourselves, in the great, natural life cycle. There dwells an underlying faith, a certainty that this season's planting, pruning, and nourishing will be rewarded.*

Jack Lenor Larsen

Jack Lenor Larsen was already emerging as an icon in the design world during the 1960s. He had studied architecture at the Cranbrook Academy in Bloomfield Hills, Michigan, with its many design associations from the 1930s. Other notable designers and architects attending Cranbrook included Charles Eames, Florence Knoll, and Benjamin Baldwin. Larsen is widely considered to be one of the most creative and inspired textile and fabric designers of this period in the United States and elsewhere.

For over fifty years his fabrics have been sought by designers all over the world. When Larsen founded his own company, it produced handwoven textiles of diverse natural yarns in random repeats. Over the years, these fabrics were developed until they came to represent the height of style and sophistication in contemporary twentieth-century domestic and commercial interior design.

In the late 1950s and during the 1960s, the State Department sent Larsen to southeast Asia, where he worked on a project designed to encourage local crafts. Since then, Larsen's work has continued to be informed and inspired by many trips within Asia and to India, Africa, Europe, and South America. As a result, he has become one of the world's foremost authorities on traditional and contemporary crafts. Having gained his reputation for innovation in fabric design, Larsen is one of only two designers to have been given the ultimate accolade of an exhibition at the Palais du Louvre. He is the author of nine books written over thirty years, a scholar and curator, with exhibitions on textiles and fabrics in museums in America and abroad, a world traveler, and a gardener. Larsen's extraordinary and wide-ranging career has brought him into contact with leading twentieth-century architects such as Edward Larrabee Barnes,

**Far right** *Larsen plays brilliantly with perspective and a single color in his Red Garden: Japanese ceremonial red for bark-stripped cedar posts and the blue-red of azaleas. The focal point is a stoneware jar by Toshiko Takaezu.*

## GARDEN STATISTICS

**Designer:** Jack Lenor Larsen

**Area:** 16 acres

**Climate:** Zones 4–5

**Soil type:** Sandy

**Aspect:** South-north and west

**Date of completion:** Ongoing

**Number of gardeners:** 1 full-time plus contractors

Charles Forberg, Louis Kahn, I. M. Pei, Minoru Yamasaki, and the offices of Skidmore, Owings and Merrill. His work is in permanent collections in New York, Chicago, Philadelphia, Amsterdam, Copenhagen, Edinburgh, London, Paris, and Zurich.

A few years ago, we began to hear about an unusual and brilliant garden on Long Island. It was on a very overcast day in 1995 that we saw Larsen's garden at the LongHouse. His design shows what can happen to a fairly unpromising piece of East Coast American woodland when the designer has knowledge, verve, a superb eye, and experience of a locale. Before buying the LongHouse, Larsen had owned an adjacent property called the Round House. This was his first house and garden. It taught him what would flourish in the dry, sandy soil.

When making his new garden, Larsen incorporated the Red Garden, one of the most striking features from the earlier property. It consists of an allée of parallel cedar posts painted fiery red reminiscent of the *torii* gates of Japan. The posts are underplanted with various red azaleas chosen for their vibrant, clashing colors. Purple plum and red barberry complete the design. The focal point of the allée is a large, exquisite stoneware jar by the potter Toshiko Takaezu. The arrangement of the posts creates a heightened perspective, making the jar appear much farther away than it really is.

The entry to the LongHouse and its gardens is through an allée of impressive Cryptomeria japonica running from the roadside to the turning circle at the gatehouse. The extended, crossed wood posts of the gatehouse, as well as the gable ends of the house, call up images of the wooden structures in the seventh-century Shinto temple precinct at Ise, Japan. Larsen's architectural use of them here is but another reflection of his aesthetic of simplicity and restraint, whether in his textile designs, houses, or gardens.

The patch of land Larsen bought for the LongHouse was former farmland that had been left fallow for fifty years. Bittersweet, poison ivy, and wild grapevines five to six inches in diameter had rollicked up the bare trunks of sad-looking pine trees, with their tall heads pointing downward from lack of sun. On the credit side of the "garden-potential" ledger, there were some old oaks, groves of beech, some stands of indigenous dogwood, 2½ acres or so of blueberries, and, within a shady area, a large plot of native ginseng. A usable depth of leaf mold had formed over the sandy soil since the land had not been worked for many years. Larsen thought that the most positive existing features were the dead-straight banks that had evolved as a result of the farmer piling up earth as field borders when the land had been actively farmed. Another advantage was the site of the house, which is a thousand feet from the road.

**Below** *The master plan by Larsen of the LongHouse and its gardens.*

**Left** *The lawn amphitheater with its simple rough wooden seats where Larsen organizes performances.*

**Below** *Stucco pillars frame a square pool and pond. The pillars support finials of a horizontal variation on the ends of the LongHouse roof.*

Further basic planting and ground preparation for the new garden included clearing saplings, vines, and fallen trees and opening up the woodland paths and a couple of grassy meadows with a JCB backhoe. Larsen planted several thousand Canadian hemlocks, bare-rooted and cheaply priced, on the banks. He then ordered hundreds of small beech, birch, dogwood, and winterberry to the same specification. To counter drought conditions, he installed a third of a mile of irrigation piping. The gypsy moth attacked twice in as many years, but he was able to save the very young beech trees. Larsen was still maintaining his garden at the nearby Round House, which was time-consuming in terms of the new project. Bamboo, cryptomeria, western cedars, and Pfitzer junipers were all moved from the Round House to the new LongHouse garden. Being a practical person, he collected mountain laurel from new housing developments.

Larsen had wanted a large pond in a spot about five feet lower than ground level. A conservation team advised him that there would be insufficient run-off, so—ever creative and adaptable—he turned the area into a bowl-shaped amphitheater, inspired by the ancient ring forts he had seen in western Ireland. The grassed ring is not only an amphitheatre: the lower side of the bowl has an outer earth ring to block both the view of the road and the sounds resonating from it. He has planted thousands of snowdrops and crocuses inspired by what he calls the "*millefleur* spring

159

plantings" at Hidcote in Gloucestershire, England. The bowl, sadly, looked wonderful the first spring, but then the bulbs became a banquet for the voles in the second year. By contrast, the grass bowl's acoustics were fine, and the first concert to take place in it featured a jazz combo led by Larry Rivers. The amphitheater has also been used for dance performances, readings, and installations of contemporary sculpture. When the tough zoysia grass finally covers it, there will be no need to water, mow, or weed.

this raised garden. Mat-forming plants, including four varieties of a low-growing and spreading juniper, beach plums, and dune grass, cover the sand-covered slopes. There is a wide section on the top of the bank reserved for santolina, lavender, and other drought-resistant plants.

The LongHouse covers an area of thirteen thousand square feet. It has a total of eighteen spaces on four levels. The raised main floor of the house has another advantage (Le Corbusier's term

**Below** *Ornamental grasses edge the pond at the LongHouse.*

On arrival at the house, the visitor is confronted with the sand hillocks that form the Dune Garden—considered a necessity by Larsen since he rarely goes now to the nearby beaches. Here he has planted a range of maritime plants and grasses. The dunes and the planting together constitute a superb reference to Long Island Sound and the proximity of the Atlantic Ocean. Even more exciting than the Dune Garden is the Raised Bank Garden, which is on the level of the second-floor rooms of the house. A bridge connects the solarium and dining room to

"piloti" would work as a definition for the pillars). It creates a large, free undercroft space that can be used as an extension to the living space provided by the main house—as an outdoor dining room perhaps, or simply as a shady space on a hot summer's day.

The undercroft gives a view of the two main axes of the garden. Perpendicular to the house is a fifty-foot black lap pool, and in line with the house is more water in the form of a large pond. From the upper floor of the house, the pink garden can be seen on the other side of the water: the pale birch trunks, a group of maples specially selected for their splendid fall color, and, perhaps most attractive of all, the masonry and bronze forms of Grace Knowlton's giant spherical sculptural shapes wonderfully spaced on the lawn by the pond.

When we first saw the LongHouse garden, Larsen had just finished creating an incredibly imaginative maze out of sunflowers. In late spring, a rabbit could have looked over the tops of the young plants. By early autumn, when the mature plants had reached

**Below left** *Blown-glass balls by Dale Chihuly. On the left is* Opaque Float with Gold Leaf and Green Lines, *1995. The ball on the right is* Midnight Blue Float, *1992. The wood-and-bronze construction in the background is* Gateway Bell, *1993, by Toshiko Takaezu.*

**Below** *Untitled, 1989, by Pavel Opocensky made of Pennsylvania granite.*

their full height of eight feet, he would have been well and truly dwarfed.

Edgar J. Kaufmann Jr. is a knowledgeable and enthusiastic supporter of the arts in the United States. His father commissioned Frank Lloyd Wright to envision the magnificent family house in Pennsylvania, Fallingwater. Kaufmann comments on Larsen:

> Jack Lenor Larsen's career is a stupendous success story, spreading to the corners of the earth, integrated with modern society, and amply recognized.

*[Michelangelo's] Campidoglio in Rome is a demonstration far beyond the resources of painting of what architecture and sculpture fundamentally, unequivocally, are. He affirms that architecture is a space, an environment . . . It says that the human act creates the environment, shapes the human world.*

Vincent Scully

# Arata Isozaki

## Tsukuba Civic Center, Tsukuba Science City, Ibaragi Prefecture, Japan

**Far right** *Traditional Japanese garden elements of stone and water employed in a splendidly artificial, postmodern design by Arata Isozaki, one of Japan's greatest contemporary architects.*

Tsukuba Scientific New Town was part of a comprehensive plan, one of several of its kind, aimed at drawing areas of activity and population away from the dense conurbation of approximately twelve million residents in Tokyo, one of the largest cities in the world. Tsukuba is a 6,750-acre site for a community of 120,000, some forty miles northeast of Tokyo. As with so many new towns, it was intended to be culturally and economically self-sufficient.

Development work began in 1966. By the late 1970s, it was clear that the plans for the new town had not been properly realized, despite a new university on the site. The large university buildings and high-rise apartment buildings of "the academic new town" appeared to be abandoned, and the Le Corbusier–inspired buildings looked inhumane and shabby. Furthermore, a population of only thirty thousand had been attracted to Tsukuba—a quarter of the projected figure. Many university and research institute employees preferred to make the two-hour commute to work from Tokyo each day. In an attempt to improve this situation, the Housing and Urban Development Corporation of Japan asked ten architectural practices to submit plans for a new civic center. They were asked not to submit designs for the development but to respond to the corporation's brief with written analyses. In his report, Arata Isozaki emphasized the site's many problems and suggested improvements. By attacking the difficulties openly and frankly, he won the commission. *Time* magazine refers to Isozaki as the international star of Japanese architecture, an opinion supported by many projects including an Olympic gymnasium in Barcelona; the Museum of Contemporary Art in Los Angeles;

the University of Art and Design in Tokyo; an arts center in Minnesota; and the Walt Disney corporate headquarters in Orlando, Florida.

In the late 1980s, Isozaki submitted his innovative master plan for the Paternoster Square project near St. Paul's in London, but Prince Charles wanted, and is getting, his neo-Georgian way. Isozaki acknowledges that the influence of the West on his work is as important as that of the traditions of his native Japan:

> You must understand our values. Our values, the first cultural things, when we were very young, came from the United States. Every kind of cultural high standard—rock music, architecture, technology, computers, cars, everything—came from the United States. Today, Japan makes cars and everything much better, but it doesn't matter. The first things we learned were Western. Even the books in the college libraries were Western.

In the design for Tsukuba, as in that for the Los Angeles Museum of Contemporary Art, Isozaki "quotes" from earlier historical styles of both Japan and the West. This is a major characteristic of postmodernism and a notable trait of Isozaki's work.

When he was interviewed in 1987, Isozaki referred to two types of quotation: "just copying traditional elements on the surface of a building. This is a method which is fashionable in Tokyo and Japan. They copy tradition." He prefers to use "a transformed quotation," which he describes as a parody:

> Parody is not directly using the patterns of the past, but using the ideas, the same ideas with a different means. Pastiche is just transporting the past style to the present, but if we can use those quoted elements in some very different ways, it makes something more interesting.

Isozaki admits to having quoted a long list of architects, both historical and contemporary: Giulio Romano, Michelangelo, Claude-Nicolas Ledoux, Otto Wagner, Richard Meier, Michael Graves, Charles Moore, Aldo Rossi, Hans Hollein, Peter Cook, Adalberto Libera, Philip Johnson, Leon Krier,

Lawrence Halprin, Ettore Sottsass, and many others.

The Tsukuba Civic Center was finally completed in 1983. At its center is the totally artificial, hard landscape of the sunken forum. Here, Isozaki quotes from the paving patterns created by Michelangelo in the Campidoglio in Rome:

> I quoted Michelangelo, but with everything completely reversed. For example, the black and white of the pattern is reversed, and levels are opposite. The Campidoglio is on a hilltop, but at Tsukuba, it's the lowest point. Convex becomes concave. It is a quotation, but not direct.

An overlapping, layered, modernist grid of walkways embraces the forum. It also creates a contrast with the other elements leading down into

**Below** *Humanizing allées of trees edge the layered stone grids in the oval sunken forum in the center of Tsukuba.*

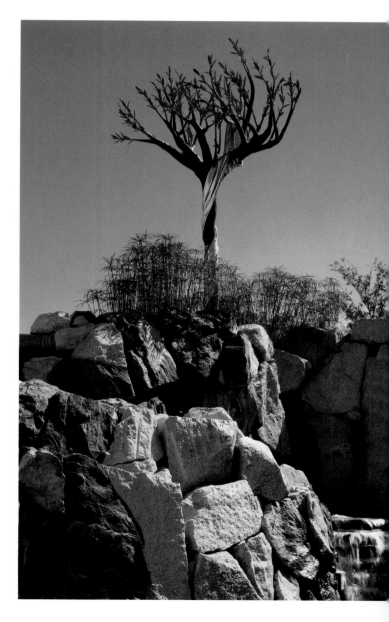

the space. Naturalistic boulders edge wide stairs that connect the forum with the upper areas and also serve as an amphitheater. The boulders also frame the rushing cascade of water that falls down from a large upper pool. Isozaki has reduced the torrent to a narrow rill as it passes through the Campidoglio paving pattern. At the exact center of this pattern, it disappears from sight into an opening. This corresponds to the central point of the Campidoglio, the site of one of the few bronze equestrian statues that has survived from Roman times, that of Emperor Marcus Aurelius.

When he was asked about his use of space in the forum, Isozaki said:

> I made the center space simply a space—a void; I portrayed a metaphor in which all the usual spatial arrangements are reversed or inverted. Everything is situated around a void, descending and then vanishing into the oblivion at the center.

Isozaki has also included allées of trees that march through the layered grid of thoroughfares above the sunken forum. The trees have begun to provide a soft, green ribbon of leaf, which contrasts with the rigorous architecture.

# Raymond Jungles

## Garden of the Colorful Corporate Headquarters, Boca Raton, Florida

*The plant is, to the landscape artist, not only a plant—rare, unusual, ordinary, or doomed to disappearance —but it is also a color, a shape, a volume, or an arabesque in itself.*

Roberto Burle Marx

The Brazilian artist and landscape designer Roberto Burle Marx is considered one of the most important influences on landscape architecture this century. A wonderful ceramic mural by Burle Marx is on the far side of the swimming pool in the garden of the Jungles-Yates house in Key West, Florida. We first saw this garden in January 1998, and it was a stunning introduction to the tropical landscape designs of Raymond Jungles and his wife and collaborator, the artist-muralist Debra Lynn Yates.

Over a thirteen-year period, they had both visited Brazil in order to work and study with Burle Marx. Jungles recalls, "I was really struggling between architecture and landscape architecture when I read a book about Roberto. It blew me away. He seemed to be able to fuse structured design and nature."

The legendary Brazilian has been credited by some academic pundits on the landscape as *the* prime mover of the modern garden in the twentieth century. He always thought of himself as primarily a painter, just as Noguchi viewed himself as a sculptor and Barragán saw himself as an architect, but like them, he became obsessed by landscape design. In his youth during the 1920s, Burle Marx was a student painter in Berlin. Here he visited the Dahlem Botanical Gardens, where he discovered the native plants of Brazil that were to become his lifelong passion. The plants that Burle Marx used in his designs were chosen from indigenous tropical species. His selection was shaped and defined by his vision as a painter. The influence of artists such Arp, Miró, and Gorky can all be seen in his designs.

Burle Marx's twentieth-century architect collaborators were Le Corbusier, Lucio Costa, and Oscar Niemeyer. With the latter he designed landscapes in their Brazil's enormous, purpose-built capital,

**Far right** *Giant variegated yellow bamboo is a counterpoint to the mural by Debra Lynn Yates, who describes Miami as the place "where the U.S. meets the Third World, more than anywhere else in America."*

## GARDEN STATISTICS

**Client:** Withheld at client's request

**Budget:** $200,000

**Designer:** Raymond Jungles

**Artist:** Debra Lynn Yates

**Concrete patinater:** David Shankman

**Area:** 31,000 square feet

**Climate:** Zone 11

**Soil type:** Sand on rock

**Aspect:** East

**Date of completion:** 1993

Brasilia. Other creations from his multifaceted range of designs are the abstract sculptural parkways and wave-shaped patterns of the promenade of Copacabana—further evidence that a good designer can design anything.

In his garden designs, Burle Marx planted large drifts, swathes, and massings of native Brazilian plants in bold curves, free-form biomorphic shapes that make a great visual impact. The planting often contrasts with the precise, geometric plan and paths of his gardens, as well as the modern architecture to which they are pendant. Burle Marx said that "A garden is the result of an arrangement of natural materials according to aesthetic laws; interwoven throughout are the artist's outlook on life, his past experiences, his affections, his attempts, his mistakes, and his successes."

Both Burle Marx and Jungles have been obsessed by the dramatic "palette" of tropical plants. Plants that are classified as hot, glasshouse, or conservatory subjects in the temperate climates of North America and Europe "rollick away" in Jungles's designs. Architectural leaf shapes and the hot colors of tropical flowers make his gardens singular. "Plants are the stars in my landscapes," says Jungles. Some of the plants that he most commonly uses are saw palmetto, sabal, fishtail, coconut, fan, and *veitchii* palms; many types

and sizes of bamboo; leather and firecracker ferns; cycads, oleanders and bananas; orchids; all sorts of bromeliads; purple, coral, and pink bouganvillea; many colors of lantana; multicolored birds-of-paradise; white and pink crinum lilies; single and double-flowered hibiscus; and silk floss trees. From Brazil, Jungles has imported species to grow in his Key West garden and then be planted in his Florida projects: drunken sailor tree, bismarckia palms, and traveler's tree are but a few examples.

Raymond Jungles and Debra Lynn Yates were commissioned as a team to work on the Colorful Corporate Headquarters, the subject of this case study. Some of the main objectives of the garden were to create a design for corporate offices that reflected the owner's commitment to the arts; to make areas where the employees could eat, smoke, and relax on their breaks from work; to create a more distinctive and noticeable entry point to the building; and to lead the visitors to elevators that would take them to second-floor offices. There were to be garden views from all of the offices, and the design had to integrate the highly colored art pieces inside the building with the garden, creating a cohesive experience. Finally, the headquarters was to be a distinctive presence on the busy highway, the adjacent US 1, the Dixie Highway.

Jungles and Yates worked closely with each other and with the owner, his architect, and the design consul-tant on all of the hard landscape elements: the owner's garden, the employee garden, the water garden, the serpentine wall, and the walkways and built-in benches, plus the planting, lighting, address graphics, and the all-important irrigation.

There were special problems relating to the existing site. The first was the fifteen-foot projection of the building's second floor. On the first site visit, the half-dead plants and mundane paving beneath the overhang were immediately striking. The relation between building and parking lot had to be improved, and space for a water garden and palm trees found from it. The undistinguished, multitenant architecture of the building also had to be improved and made more memorable by the new design. Jungles and Yates took their cue for the exterior from the art collection inside, designing colorful murals and bold planting.

Jungles and Yates were extremely pleased with their revamp of the Colorful Corporate Headquarters. The employees make full use of the redesigned outdoor space, and, perhaps highest praise of all, even the building inspectors became very complimentary on their various visits to the gardens.

**Below** *The once dark and dreary undercroft of a company's headquarters transformed with robust planting and mosaic walls.*

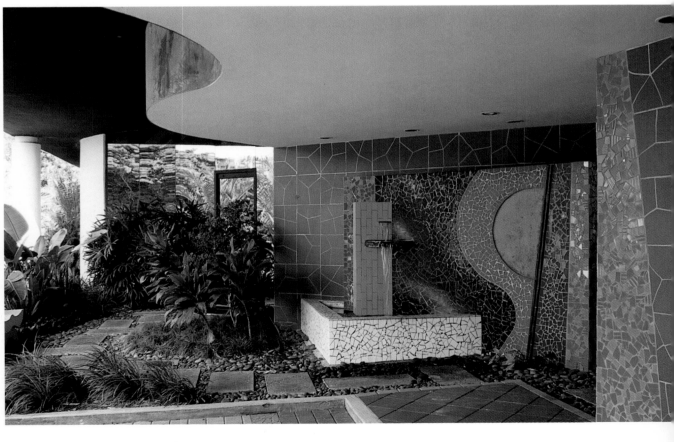

*My hope is that my intuitive method of working manifests so that people will connect viscerally with the work in a way that makes it their own, and provides a lens for their own vision. I cannot define what that will be exactly. Each person has an individual response.*

Kathryn Gustafson

# Kathryn Gustafson

## Fragments of Garden History, Terrasson-La-Villedieu, Dordogne, France

*Far right: This spectacular, three-thousand-foot-long, gilded aluminum ribbon leads visitors through the oak grove of Fragments of Garden History.*

During the spring of 1992, in the region of Perigord, France, the unusually visionary town fathers of Terrasson-La-Villedieu decided to organize a competition for the design of a new public park and gardens. They invited Kathryn Gustafson, an American landscape architect with practices in Paris, Seattle, and London, to participate in a competition for a public garden. The site was a beautiful, forested hillside overlooking the town. *Continent Imaginaire* was the title of the brief. It specified a series of designs to be based on various historic gardens of the world, with a greenhouse information center as its main public focus.

The fifteen-acre site has spectacular views over the town and the valley of the River Vezere. The slope is on a one-in-four gradient, and there is a network of caves in the ancient oak forest. Maple and acacia have colonized the forest edge, and in the open field areas there is a diversity of indigenous plants. Water from a group of cistern wells and an intricate and historic drainage system serve the central fountain and hospital of the town.

The town of Terrasson, which has six thousand citizens, financed the initial phase of the competition. The later phases were underwritten by a broad-based group of sponsors: Terrasson, the province of Dordogne, the Region of Aquitaine, the nearby town of Brive-la-Gaillard, the Ministry of Culture, the Ministry of Tourism and the European Community. The initial budget was 10 million francs ($1.6 million) for the garden, and 4 million francs ($640,000) for the buildings. Kathryn Gustafson, the leading landscape architect on the project, worked with Ian Ritchie, an English architect. The complexity and richness of the garden is the result of collaboration between Gustafson, Ritchie, and

## GARDEN STATISTICS

**Client:** Municipality of Terrasson-La-Villedieu, France

**Budget:** FF10 million

**Designer:** Kathryn Gustafson

**Area:** 15 acres

**Climate:** Temperate

**Soil type:** Alkaline mixed

**Aspect:** North

**Date of completion:** 1995

**Number of gardeners:** 4 plus 1 part-time

other landscape architects, artists, and garden historians from Australia and France. A better, more specific, and poetic name evolved for the project: its name was changed to "Fragments of Garden History."

Despite the diversity of its members, the group agreed that history cannot be, and should not be, re-created. Basic elements of garden history were to be translated into contemporary forms. Think of a book on classical architecture — Vitruvius perhaps — with facades, floor plans, and orders of columns. Having studied the elements, buildings in the classical style have even more meaning and coherence for us. At Terrasson, we see contemporary design concepts inspired by the high points of many centuries of garden history. The fragmented presentation enhances visitors' interest regarding gardens of the past. Imagine grass-covered, earth-form amphitheater terraces reminiscent of Claremont in eighteenth-century Britain, add the long canals and serial water jets of the *regulier* style of seventeenth-century France, and bring in the slanting, stone water slides of the sixteenth-century Mogul summer palace in Kashmir. All of these images and many others are brought from the depths of visitors' memories and into the foreground of their immediate experience while they explore this new garden.

The opening design note of the gardens is the Axis of the Wind. It is a line of wind vanes on slender fifty-foot metal masts. Omnidirectional ball joints connect the vanes to the masts, showing not only wind direction but also wind turbulence. On each mast there is a bell. The visitor not only sees but hears the wind.

The sonorous, "singing" wind masts lead from the parking lot and entrance path. At the entrance to the

garden, the visitor catches a first glimpse of the trompe l'oeil of parallel land forms running across the main clearing at the top of the site. The area is planted with high grass and white roses. The main path, edged with clipped box, slopes up to the Elements Garden and the Glasshouse Fragment. This is an extremely simple, innovative glasshouse with a flat, high-tech glass roof that, when viewed from above in certain lights, appears to be a small lake. The laminated, toughened glass is secured with "phantom fixtures" developed by the Ritchie team. The sturdy walls are made from stacked *gabions*, wire mesh boxes filled with stones. The glasshouse is an exhibition space, a bookstore, and a café-bar. It serves as a landscape interpretation center for the gardens, providing visitors with a historical background and visual images of the designers' sources of inspiration.

Adjacent to the glasshouse is another large clearing. Here the land has been modeled into an amphitheater of grass and steel. The area provides spectacular views of the town, the river valley, and the Rose and Water Gardens. The roses are planted to grow up, over, and down a 3,280-foot steel arbor, creating a suspended tapestry of flowers that floats down the hill toward the Water Garden.

The pools in the Water Garden represent the moment in which water, formerly used for agricultural irrigation, became a source of sensuous pleasure in

**Right** *A view of Terrasson-La-Villedieu. The glasshouse in the foreground was designed by Ian Ritchie, the noted contemporary British architect.*

**Above** *The wind mast is fifty feet high. Changes in the direction of the wind are reflected by the action of an omnidirectional ball joint and by the ringing of the bell attached to each mast.*

**Above** *Grassed earth tiers and steel benches form an amphitheater set among a grove of existing and newly planted trees with views of the town of Terrasson.*

**Left** *Plan for Fragments of Garden History*

the garden. The Pathway of Fountains leads to a cruciform four-square design—the most ancient form of garden plan. On a sunny day, rainbows play in the water, which shoots out from fifteen randomly placed jets rising from the large, rectangular pool.

Beyond the Water Garden is an enclosed vault of flowering trees leading toward the Topiary Room. Nearby is a large square of grass used for temporary landscape designs. A designer or artist will create a new pattern or design in the area each year. The design for the first year was a painted garden called "Ephemeral Tracing." Low lights in a grid pattern illuminate the area at night.

The return path leads through a large, abstract topiary into the Sacred Forest of the oak grove. Leading the visitor through the oak grove is a three-thousand-foot-long thin, aluminum, gold-leafed ribbon, weaving in and out of the tree canopy fifteen feet above the path. Set alongside the gilded ribbon are four small gardens that explore the role of particular plants chosen from the indigenous vegetation.

These gardens show their transformation through hybridization; the species found here are the Montpelier maple, rhododendron, azalea, and ferns and moss.

Gustafson came to landscape from fashion design: the molding of wool jersey versus the molding of clay. The critical first sketches for a landscape design are made in clay, and the resulting bas-relief is the inspiration for the project. Large-scale landscapes for the Shell and L'Oreal headquarters, and the Plaza of Human Rights, adjacent to the new cathedral by Mario Botta at Evry near Paris, are three other major achievements. Gustafson has collaborated with Neil Porter and John Lyall on the New Crystal Palace Park Project in south London; they have received partial funding for the first phase of park—the restoration section. Gustafson and her collaborators have worked on this project against huge opposition. The designs respect the nineteenth-century remnants of the park while bringing to a partially derelict site exciting contemporary twentieth-century buildings and a landscape for the public to enjoy.

**Far left** *A dramatic variety of water designs. The water steps in the foreground evoke a sixteenth-century Mogul garden in Kashmir or Lahore.*

**Left** *An apparently endless formal canal echoes the seventeenth-century château gardens of André Le Nôtre.*

**Above** *Gustafson's field of water jets in the Water Garden.*

# Fernando Caruncho

## The Wheat Parterre, Mas de les Voltes, Ampurdan, Catalonia, Spain

*In order to travel into the future, it is necessary to walk toward the pure clarity of the past.*

Fernando Caruncho, inspired by Petrarch

**Far right** *Caruncho's design is a formal masterpiece using vines, olives, and wheat, the plants that were fundamental to the economy of the ancient Mediterranean. A huge circular pool is the focal point within a wheat parterre.*

Ancient agriculture meets formal contemporary garden design in the late twentieth century. Wheat, olive trees, cypresses, water, and grass are the elements of this astonishing and original case study. Fernando Caruncho is classically educated, as can be seen from any of his designs, which combine profound simplicity with extraordinary sophistication. He came to garden design while studying classical philosophy at the University of Madrid. He thinks of himself as a gardener, not a landscape architect or a designer. He made his first garden for an uncle (in a house by Richard Neutra) when he was twenty-one, and he knew then that he had found his vocation.

In additional to the classical philosophers, Caruncho also venerates Descartes and Goethe. Rousseau from the same period but on the opposite side of the philosophical equation—is an anathema, as are the unnaturally "natural" English parklands of Capability Brown. And of course, he finds loathsome and boring the flowery English cottage and manor house garden style, as typified by those "good taste," book-writing, sub–Gertrude Jekyll, English granny gardeners. Caruncho says that his designs are a constant attempt "to capture the light (vibration lumineuse)" in the garden space through a formal setting of the simplest elements: "Everything in a Spanish garden is founded on how you deal with the light." The rich history of Spanish gardens, which display the combined influence of the Moors and the Italian Renaissance, also informs his designs. Caruncho's favorite historic gardens are the Alhambra Palace gardens in Granada; the Boboli gardens of the Pitti Palace, Florence; and André Le Nôtre's Château Vaux-le-Vicomte, south of Paris. Contemporary aestheticheroes of his are the minimalist

**Above** *The contour lines in the master plan of the Wheat Parterre indicate the subtle grading of the slope: the parterres disappear, becoming one field of wheat.*

architects Louis Kahn, Tadao Ando, and Luis Barragán. Until 1998, when he was commissioned by Ricardo Legorreta to make a garden in Florida, Caruncho had worked principally in Spain and France. He has also been commissioned to design the garden of the new Spanish embassy in Tokyo.

Caruncho's design concept for this project was wheat, one of human-kind's most ancient cereal-crops, used as the basis of a formal parterre of soil and water, to be built on a farm in northern Spain. The Parterre contains echoes of both the agricultural and the architectural history of Spain, which were both primary influences. Among the highly developed Islamic arts and sciences brought to the country by the Moors in the eighth century were advanced agricultural and irrigation methods.

These innovations also made possible the creation of the great gardens of Cordoba and Granada, such as the Alhambra, with designs based on the formal style that had originated in Persia. The parterres of the seventeenth century were also a source of inspiration. The Wheat Parterre in early spring resembles the *parterre à l'anglaise* or *gazon coupé*, which was

formed from designs made in cut sod.

When asked about his spiritual home, Caruncho replies that it is in Tuscany. He now realizes that the Wheat Parterre, with its Italianate qualities, has been unconsciously inspired by the paintings of Piero della Francesca. Just think of the coffered squares of the ceiling in the cool geometric painting *The Flagellation of Christ*. Late in life, della Francesca became so obsessed with linear and mathematical theory that he gave up painting altogether.

Caruncho sees the garden as a mirror of the universe: "I strive to arrange a space that invites reflection and inquiry by allowing the light to delineate geometries, perspectives, and symmetries." In his gardens, the harmonies of the enclosure express for the spectator a sense of order and balance. He thinks that gardens can also narrate some sense of the history of ideas, arousing rather the same feeling as a rose window in a Gothic cathedral; the cathedral in Ghent is a particular inspiration.

The Wheat Parterre was conceived as the quintessential landscape of the Mediterranean, since wheat, olives, and wine have been produced on this land since ancient times. Caruncho wanted the garden to be connected with the context of the farmland and faithful to the ancient culture. The brilliance lies in the simple minimalism of his late-twentieth-century concept.

When Caruncho arrived on the site in northern Spain, the large stone farmhouse or *masia*, with its ancient tile roof and splendid strong-arched loggia, had been completely restored, but the land was exhausted:

> The soil had been depleted by centuries of overwork until nothing would grow here. It was a monumental task to replenish the land. We had to bring in 565,000 cubic feet of new soil, but we knew we were not only creating a garden but restoring a millennia-old landscape.

To enclose the wonderful wheat and carp pond parterres and the rest of the garden, Caruncho has planted stands of bamboo, groves of evergreen oaks, and orchards of cherry, apple, pomegranate, and fig. The four square carp ponds are set in grass and enclosed by shallow terraces of grapevines. Screened by a terrace wall is a kitchen garden and a rose garden for cutting, and the only other color nearby is from water lilies in a raised pool at the base of a ruined watch tower. These are the only flowers Caruncho has included anywhere in the design. He maintains firmly:

> This is an agricultural garden . . . here a flower—any flower—would look out of place. For flower-filled borders one can go to Sissinghurst, but the landscape of the Mediterranean needs something quite different. This is a garden of forms, geometry, and light.

This is borne out by the seasons and by work in the garden. Caruncho is at his most poetic on this subject:

> In the summer, the wheat is tall and golden and the great plots sway gently in the wind. There is fruit in the orchard. Autumn brings the grape harvest and the cutting of the wheat. In winter the earth is plowed and sown and marked by wonderful patterns. And in the spring, once again, all is a sea of green. What could be more beautiful or ennobling than producing flour from wheat, wine

from the vines, oil from the olives, and fruit from the trees? In a sense this is the first garden, a garden with all the purity of a Platonic ideal.

Late afternoon in this garden in any season, when the western sun is low in the clear Mediterranean sky, the carp ponds shimmer darkly or reflect a passing

cloud. The olive trees tremble with the silvery underside of their leaves catching the light, the wheat is golden, and the cypresses cast strong, dark shadows across the immaculate lawns of the paths. All these elements are caught in the light-filled space that Caruncho describes in all of his gardens—*caja de luz*—"box of light"—and here, it is a wondrous illumination.

**Above** *A cross section of the Mas de les Voltes design reveals the relationship between the imposing farmhouse, the parterres of wheat and water, and the verticals of the olives and cypresses.*

**Above** *A line of tall cypresses along the main drive gives onto a view of the Wheat Parterre. The parterre is bounded by lawn paths and ancient olive trees imported from Italy.*

# Walter Beck and Lester Collins

## Innisfree Gardens, Millbrook, New York

*I will arise and go now,*
*and go to Innisfree,*
*And a small cabin build there,*
*of clay and wattles made . . .*

W. B. Yeats, *The Lake Isle of Innisfree*

When it was first built, Innisfree had a "cup garden" that demanded the attention of two full-time gardeners just to maintain the moss steps, which could be walked on only once a week. The steps led to an exquisite Chinese teahouse, a construction hardly congruent to the small cabin of clay and wattle descibed in Yeats's beautiful poem.

Marion and Walter Beck, who created this amazingly spiritual garden, tried out various names for it, all Chinese-inspired: Garden of the Seven Gates and Way to the Clouds were both contenders. To friends and the locals of Millbrook, however, it has always been Innisfree, the name inspired by W. B. Yeats's lines.

The garden was created over a period of about fifty years. It is included as a case study because of its use of the "stuff" landscape architects and designers shape, improve, and make more expressive: earth, rocks, water, trees, and shrubs. Innisfree is an object lesson in the timelessness of the appeal of simplicity in the landscape.

The two-hundred-acre site, with its forty-acre lake, was found by the Becks in the mid-1920s. She was heiress to an iron fortune, and he was a painter obsessed by the design principles of Chinese painting. They started to make the garden in 1930. After Walter Beck's death in 1954, the garden continued to evolve under the care of Lester Collins, a friend of Beck's and a landscape architect captivated by the gardens of China and Japan.

Both Beck and Collins were drawn to the notion of a garden created from a piece of the natural landscape. They believed that the viewer should be led to experience the moment, the now, of particular parts of it. Their credo was to build the essence rather than the copy.

**Far right** *An autumn view of the lake at Innisfree, which is bounded by a series of traditional, Chinese-inspired cup gardens. Regarding her late husband's work, Petronella Collins said, "The lake is natural, but please be assured that everything else is not. Lester fiddled with everything."*

### GARDEN STATISTICS

**Designer:** Walter Beck and Lester Collins

**Area:** 182 acres

**Climate:** Zone 5

**Soil type:** Neutral to acid

**Aspect:** Southeast

**Date of completion:** Ongoing

**Number of gardeners:** 5

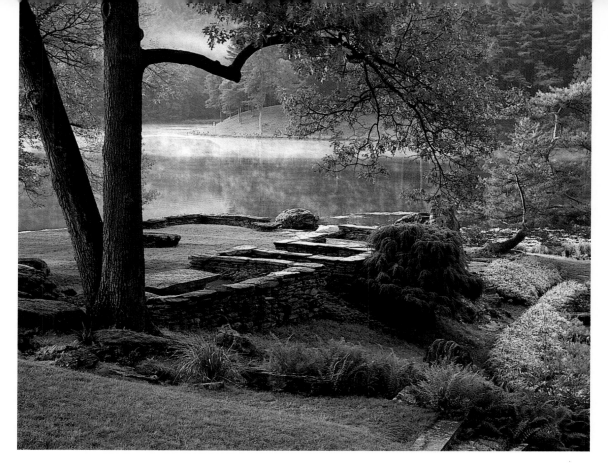

**Right** *The Point, the southernmost promontory on the lake, with stone seats designed by Beck. He created the main path around the lake to connect the cup gardens.*

**Below** *A hilltop reservoir feeds this serpentine stream in one of the many cup gardens edging the lake.*

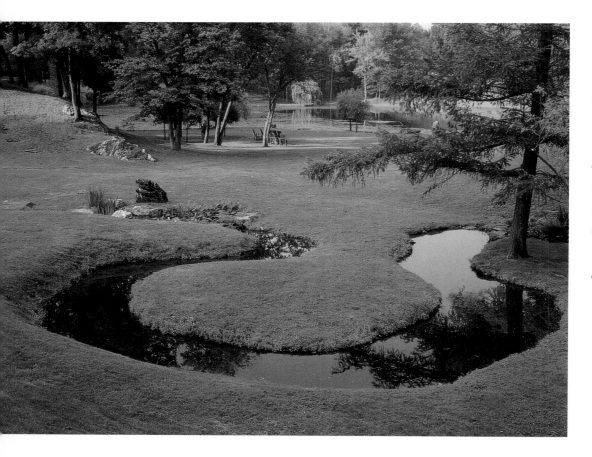

landscape paintings of the eighth-century Tang Dynasty poet, painter, and garden-builder Wang Wei. He is said by art historians to have been one of the greatest landscape painters and is also credited with the "invention" of the Chinese style of monochrome landscape painting. This style would emerge later in Japan as *sumi-e*, with the masterpieces of black ink landscapes by the painter Sesshu. In this style of painted landscape, there are defined and enclosed areas of rock and water.

Beck was also inspired by Wang Wei's poems, such as "Drifting on the Lake":

> *The autumn sky is clear into the distance*
> *The clearer so far from human habitation*
> *On a sandy shore a crane, or beyond clouds*
> *A mountain top makes my content.*
> *The limpid ripples calm and evening comes*
> *The moon shines out and I relax*
> *Tonight my single oar takes over*
> *As I drift without thought of going back.*

Water, rocks, and trees were the basic elements of the traditional Chinese garden, and later the gardens of Japan. Linguistically, the combination of the two words, water and rocks, are the Chinese characters for a landscape designer. Beck coined the term "cup garden" after a trip to London, where he discovered the

Unrolling along the horizontal plane of a scroll, the viewer sees water in the foreground, and beyond, within a series of rocky inlets, perhaps a bridge, a philosopher's teahouse, a grove of trees, an unusual rock formation, or a waterfall. These were the images that inspired Beck's Innisfree cup-garden designs. Petronella Collins, widow of Lester Collins, gave an insight into the personalities of Beck and her husband:

Walter Beck was a mystical man, no doubt about it, and he and Lester had a tremendous rapport. However, my husband was a forthright Quaker, and there were no spirits in any rocks.

Beck designed more than a dozen cup gardens around the Innisfree lake. The focal points of a Chinese painting are asymmetric and three-dimensional. The visitor walking the circuit of Innisfree experiences a constant shifting of focal points that cannot be conveyed though the static rocks and water in a Chinese black ink scroll. The circuit of changing views and perspectives reminded us of our visit to the great stroll garden of the Imperial Villa, Katsura, Kyoto.

Beck managed to capture the mystical atmosphere of Chinese landscape design on an American lake shore. He made his cup gardens by framing an area with earthworks, fences, large rocks, or trees. At ninety, overseeing work from a wheelchair, Beck completed his last cup garden. He died in 1954, and his ashes were buried near one of his waterfalls.

Beck's design approach to the garden could be summed up by a passage in the book that he wrote about painting:

One does not think in dimensions or restrictions; one is swayed by rhythms, and there is a willingness to follow wherever the experiment leads.

After his death, Beck's widow asked Collins to help her with the garden. Collins preserved the spirit of the place. The individual cup gardens had been built by Beck with no real relationship between them. Collins applied the full force of his energy and vision to making connections. He created new cup-garden incidents and a path for visitors to walk on between the gardens. Collins had long thought of Wang Wei's concept of a total landscape. At Innisfree he perceived the lake, the surrounding hills, and the three cliffs as one large cup encompassing many smaller ones. Like the great Chinese masters of the landscape, he

**Right** *A master plan of Innisfree Gardens.*

**Below** *Almost an acre of hardy pink lotus in Innisfree Lake makes a spectacular sight in July. Here they provide a backdrop for standing stones evoking traditional Taoist stone worship.*

listened to the garden itself when making his improvements, creating berms and hillocks to draw the visitor seamlessly from area to area within it. A serpentine stream sculpted in a meadow now looks as though it was hewn from the earth by a glacier many eons ago.

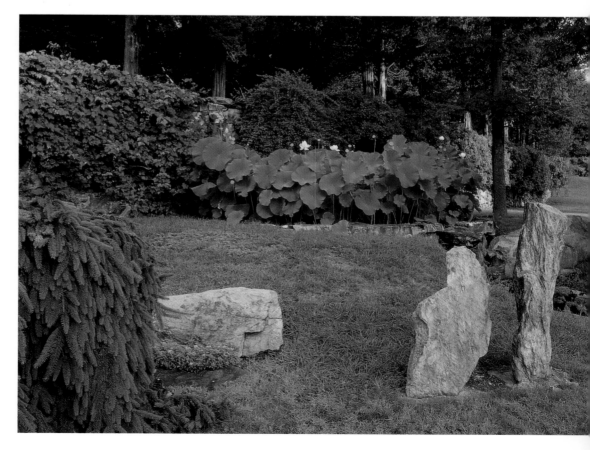

# T. Delaney & Co.

## The Leichtag Family Healing Garden, San Diego Children's Hospital, San Diego, California

*This is a garden about passion, yours, mine, and the passion of the community.*

Topher Delaney

The designs for private gardens created by T. Delaney & Co. have often emerged from the past lives of its clients. Topher Delaney calls this part of the client brief "the personal narrative," and it is a key element in the evolving design. The result of this approach is a personalized or "client-specific" design, a variation on the late-twentieth-century concept of the "site specific" or site generated in both landscape sculpture and architecture. Delaney and her colleagues closely question a client's past and likes and dislikes, current preoccupations, and any specific interests or obsessions.

Often the designers will include in the planting plan trees, shrubs, or flowers that for various reasons remind the client of a garden they have known in the past. They become living reminders of happy times, pleasures, and events that the client has experienced. One client wanted blue lupines to rekindle memories of her last garden in Idaho. The most dramatic composition has emerged in a San Francisco hillside plot, where shattered pieces of a terrace were set asymmetrically as low-standing stones with an interplanting of blood grass. This "Garden of Divorce" became a daily reminder of the client's recent separation and her own new life. The original terrace had been laid down by her ex-husband.

Delaney has designed several healing gardens. One is at the Highland Hospital, East Oakland, in an extremely poor African-American section of the Bay Area. Another, in Palo Alto, is specifically designed for Alzheimer's patients. Delaney has just installed a large healing garden at the Beth Israel Hospital in New York. The first of these healing gardens had its genesis in Delaney's own life—an aspect of her own personal narrative. She fought and won a battle with

**Far right** *Sheltering walls enclose the Healing Garden. The rainbow-colored blades of this fantasy windmill turn to enliven the wooden birds "caged" within its supporting struts.*

---

### GARDEN STATISTICS

**Client:** San Diego Children's Hospital

**Budget:** $400,000

**Designers:** T. Delaney & Co

**Area:** 5,000 square feet

**Climate:** Sunny and dry

**Soil type:** Clay

**Aspect:** West

**Date of completion:** 1997

**Number of gardeners:** 2

**Above** *Delaney designed private spaces for the children and their families within the brightly colored perimeter walls. Palm, magnolia, and eucalyptus trees provide shade in the garden.*

**Below** *A presentation plan shows the final design development of the healing garden.*

cancer in the Marin Cancer Center near San Francisco. At the center of the building was a courtyard, a dull, soulless, concrete-walled, open space where she decided to make a perfect interior garden. Climbing plants furnished the walls; raised planters made scented plants more accessible to patients. The centerpiece is a beautiful, Japanese-inspired fountain reflecting the influence of the Orient on Californian culture. The fountain consists of two large natural stones, one that acts as a support and one that is angled down to a round, carved bowl to contain the water. Over time, the fountain has taken on a symbolic significance. Many of the patients fill their cups and glasses there, hoping that the gently flowing water will help in some way with their cure.

Healing gardens are an ancient phenomenon. In the fourth century b.c.e., Greece had healing centers or *aesclapia* devoted to the god of medicine and healing —Aesclapius. Many temples were erected to him on high mountains and near healing springs all over Greece. Three major shrines were dedicated to him. They were on the island of Kos, in the city of Pergamon, and at the temple and theater of Epidaurus, in the eastern Peloponnese south of Athens. Vincent Scully, the great American architectural historian, has made the following comment about Epidaurus and the relationship between the natural landscape of the site and its buildings:

> The whole of the universe of men and nature
> [came] together in a single quiet order to
> be [healed].

In the third century b.c.e., Aesclapius "emigrated" to Rome. Here his shrine was consecrated on the Tiber Island. There, in the tenth century, relics of Saint Bartholomew endowed a church and a hospice for healing. During the twelfth century c.e., at this hospice in Rome, the jester of King Henry II of England, Rahere, had a vision that the king must return to England and found a sister healing center there. As a result, a hospice was founded in London in 1132. Over the centuries this hospice became known as Saint Bartholomew's Hospital.

Solitude is also a vital part of the healing process. There is a need to be alone in a garden or landscape, and this is especially true of those whose lives are devoted to healing. Contact with nature and the processes of growth and renewal provide spiritual refreshment of the body and mind.

"When the doctors can't heal anymore, your heart and your soul still need to be healed, and this is the place for it": this is the deeply felt response of Deborah Burt to the San Diego Children's Hospital. She is the mother of Sam, who has had intensive treatment there. The garden is designed to offer a safe, imaginative, uplifting, and, above all, meaningful environment for convalescent and terminally ill children and their families. Periodically, the hospital staff and the families gather in the garden for a ceremony that they call "The Celebration of Life." It is an opportunity to praise the children who have died and those who are still convalescing in the hospital.

Delaney's garden is on the site of a former parking lot of the hospital. She explains the garden:

It's a place to imagine life being larger than what's existing at the moment. Most gardens are about miracles of life, but this one deviates from the traditional.

The designers have approached the elements of the garden—the colors, shapes, textures, and particularly, the scale of the features—from the viewpoint of a child. The children feel an immediate rapport with the cartoon and computer-game colors of lemon yellow, deep blue, lilac, and burnt orange that wash the sinuous, undulating walls surrounding and intersecting the garden space. The walls form a series of garden rooms with nooks and crannies where families and staff can gather in privacy.

The child's view of this fantasy world is expressed in the garden in many ways. The entrance, which establishes privacy and sanctuary, is through the giant, open-work, painted metal legs of Sam the Dinosaur. Sam is forty feet long and twenty-one feet high. He is clad with the vigorous, purple-red *Bougainvillea spectabilis* cultivar aptly named 'San Diego.'

**Left** *A jolly mosaic seahorse fountain adds the magic of splashing water to hot southern California summer days.*

**Below** *The entrance to the garden is a giant forty-foot-long climbing frame for bougainvillea called "Sam the Dinosaur."*

**Above** *This stalking mountain lion silhouette is one of many animal cutouts in the metal wall sections among the bright concrete perimeter walls. The animals cast shadows onto the swirling cement ground plane's sea and sand colors.*

This fantastical beast was named after a patient, a four-year-old boy who has had twenty operations at the hospital. Sam Burt's mother, Deborah, was a leading force in the creation of the garden, knowing first-hand the importance of it: "When your kid is hooked up to an IV drip day after day, the sound of the birds and the wind in the trees is like heaven."

Other creatures featured in the garden include a giant seahorse fountain rising from a sea-blue concrete floor gently shooting jets into shallow pools, and three hundred ceramic sea animals set into the walls. There is also a rainbow-colored windmill with mechanically driven birds inside its open structure. Within the garden, the Celestial Wall is inset with the signs of the zodiac, and the Constellation Wall is decorated with 158 glass stars glowing in the afternoon sun. Other walls have glass disks in the shape of ducks, horses, bats, and mice casting their scampering shadows on the ground and providing a focus during the day for partially sighted children. At night, the glass beasts are backlit by colored concrete

spheres representing the planets on the edge of the street so they can also be seen from the hospital windows overlooking the garden area. The garden's ground planes of crushed granite are swirls of soft, sandy ocher, yellow, blue, and teal green. These were inspired by the shore and the waves of the Pacific Ocean. There are plenty of places to sit and relax in the garden: mosaic seats, serpentine concrete benches, movable wheelbarrows with umbrellas, and "rainbow" rocks. From all of these seats, families can enjoy the medicinal plants and shrubs attractive to bees and butterflies.

Three small lawn areas are used for picnics. Shade and height are provided by mature palms and eucalyptus; large bird-of-paradise plants continue the bold colors and fantasy themes. Within the garden is a storytelling room for the hospital's resident storyteller. On its walls the shadows of animals are cast by large metal cutouts. Storytelling is another purposeful activity, anecdote as antidote to the clinical confines of the hospital, providing both a welcome distraction to the children and short-term mental solace for visiting parents. This and other areas of the garden bring to mind images from twentieth-century art based on colorful, abstract fantasy—the works of Joan Miró, Antoni Gaudí, and Niki de Saint-Phalle.

The Healing Garden in San Diego is unique in that it was built entirely from donated funds, labor, and materials. Paul Hagin, who is the director of facilities at the hospital, was responsible for much of the fund-raising. He also enlisted the help of an agency that specializes in the employment of high-school students in crisis, who built the walls dividing the different areas of the garden.

The client and contractor was the hospital, which, together with the hospital's Bereavement Committee, collaborated with designers at each stage of the design and installation. The garden is now complete, and it is has proved to be a great success. The use has been extended to severely handicapped children, and they are now able to share it with the other children and their families.

**Right** *Scented plants attract bees and butterflies to the garden. The star benches in the foreground are made of limestone and mosaic. Sam the Dinosaur can be seen in the background.*

**Below** *The Constellation Wall is set with 158 glass stars. The planets, colored concrete spheres with lights inset, bring glass star configurations inside the garden wall to life at night.*

# George Hargreaves

*You don't walk in and say, "This is my way," because if that's all it is, it's not a very good project. Landscape design expresses how our culture meets nature. It's not about architectural ideas. It's about people.*

George Hargreaves

# George Hargreaves

## Dayton Garden, Minneapolis, Minnesota

In a brilliant and mind-opening lecture on the contemporary landscape given at the Royal Institute of British Architects, London, in November 1993, George Hargreaves described his average brief: "Garbage sixty feet deep on landfill or post-industrial sites for eventual public use is where we are most often asked to design, not on idyllic, green-valley sites for corporate villas."

The search for meaning in the landscape is the key to the designs created by Hargreaves Associates. Nature and culture, culture and nature, the interplay and variations between these macro-concepts, have led George Hargreaves toward his interpretation of landscape architecture. He sculpts the earth and envisions forms in the land of a site. Initially, in the early part of the design process, he seeks shapes either on, in, or around the site. This approach makes his team sensitive to the existing natural landscape. They can find their inspiration for the design in the configurations and contours within view of the site. A deep and thorough inquiry into the given circumstances and natural processes of a site, such as the land, the light, the shadow, the water, the wind, and the rainfall, a thorough understanding of its larger natural context, combined with research into its history, all yield shapes and design elements for a Hargreaves project. The layout that evolves from this data is not based on an earlier pattern. It is a site-generated design. In Hargreaves's view, "The truths we uncover in the analysis of environmental phenomena should be the fodder—the subject—of design."

Hargreaves Associates was established in San Francisco, California, in 1983. When Hargreaves became head of Landscape Architecture at Harvard University Graduate School of Design, a second

**Far right** *Richard Serra's* Garden Arc, *made in 1986, is set against a background of trees. The lake, the climax of the vista, can just be seen within the filigree line of trees.*

### GARDEN STATISTICS

**Client:** Kenneth and Judy Dayton

**Budget:** Withheld at clients' request

**Designer:** Hargreaves Associates

**Area:** ¾ acre

**Climate:** Midwest U.S.A.

**Soil type:** Glacial till

**Aspect:** North-south

**Date of completion:** 1997

studio was opened in Cambridge, Massachusetts. Many of the company's California projects display an ability to emphasize the elemental in the landscape. At Byxbee Park, Palo Alto, the profile of landforms was taken from distant hills. The existing site was covered in trash to a depth of sixty feet. The firm solved this problem by spreading two feet of good soil sown with native grasses and wildflowers over twelve inches of impenetrable clay sealer. At Candlestick Cultural Park, South San Francisco, strong winds and their sounds were harnessed to the concrete Wind Gate. At Prospect Green, Sacramento, a flat valley was sculpted into landforms from earth ravaged by gold dredging.

George Hargreaves has designed gardens for just two private houses. The first was a stunning series of spirals and serpentines of contrasting grasses and wildflowers, set in a forest clearing of holm oaks and mesquite. The design contrasted with a large, white stucco, angular, asymmetric modernist house—Villa Zapu—on a hillside at the end of the Napa Valley in California.

The second is the subject of this case study. It is the Dayton residence, a rectilinear modernist villa in Minneapolis, Minnesota. Its setting, overlooking some of greater Minneapolis's many lakes, recalls two other International Style villas: the Farnsworth House by Mies van der Rohe outside Chicago and its Connecticut offspring, the Glass House by Philip Johnson. This building by local architect Vincent James Associates also has echoes of the Villa Savoye, designed by Le Corbusier outside Paris.

The history of this project is rooted in the Daytons' decision to leave their house at Wayzata and move into the city. The grounds of their old home had been the setting for a modern sculpture collection. The sculptures were arranged at intervals along a path that bounded their thirteen-acre property. Many of their favorite pieces made the move into the new garden nearer the city. This slightly smaller collection included works by Siah Armajani, Scott Burton, Ellsworth Kelly, Richard Long, David Nash, Martin Puryear, Richard Serra, Joel Shapiro, and Peter Shelton. The new sculpture circuit designed by Hargreaves is on a smaller, urban scale.

Hargreaves's landscape concept is based on a series of areas that extend the indoor-outdoor, house-landscape connection already achieved by the glass walls of the main rooms of the house. From inside the house, the different areas of the garden appear as gallery spaces for the sculptures.

Arriving at the house, the visitor is led up the immaculately paved driveway of granite setts, which leads to the parking area. On the left of the driveway Hargreaves has placed three low sculpted and grassed landforms (a signature of his singular design philosophy) that he calls "elongated pyramids with an isosceles construction." The shapes, which are his opening statements in this garden, are enclosed by a right angle of small-leaved linden

trees. The sculpted ground plane subtly signals the clients' interest in contemporary sculpture. Two works, *Ferndale Ladder* and *Standing Trunk + Limb*, both by David Nash, are set asymmetrically within the grassed mounds. Hargreaves's landforms are particularly beautiful in the summer when they cast low, dark shadows from the setting sun. In the winter, the depressions between the shapes make longer-lasting, minimalist, horizontal bas-reliefs in the snow.

**Below** *Master plan of the Dayton Garden.*

When asked about the genesis of the sculptured ground plane, Hargeaves admitted that the clients were unsure about it when it was first mentioned. He suggested it again six months later, nine months later, and finally after about a year. At this point, they said that the ground work could begin. When it was half built, the Daytons became uncertain again. Once more, Hargreaves "donned his spurs," as he puts it. He finally persuaded them to accept the grassed landforms, which they could now perceive as modernist, planar, sculptural surfaces—clean and green, and right for the garden.

Hargreaves reveled in the residential scale of this project in contrast to·the large-scale, cultural, and ecological projects on reclaimed sites:

> This was a scale you can touch and feel. It wasn't fifty, one hundred or two hundred acres. It wasn't a ten-year project. It was a project that was all going to be done at one time, and I knew it was going to be done well. It was of such a scale that you could stake things out. We staked those mounds [landforms] out and tested the size of them. We staked out the lens shape [lawn plateau] and the curves. We were out there actually doing it.

Hargreaves's other major stroke with the garden footprint is the large area that the main rooms overlook. The view through the glass walls of the living room, dining room, and kitchen is out across the narrow granite terrace and grassed plateau—or lens, as Hargreaves calls it. At its farthest extreme is the elegant curve forming the edge of the plateau, the climax of the lawn. Beyond it are the lakes and their forested shores. The plateau and curved edge were worked out by the architect and Hargreaves. As he says, "It's not an arc; it is its own shape. It is a clean shape that comes from a view of the lakes."

A robust retaining wall supports it, and below the plateau is a road leading up to the house. The arc of a steel sculpture by Richard Serra is a splendid counterpoint to Hargreaves's plateau curve. Growing up from below the curve are some existing riparian hardwood trees. The gaps between the trunks give miniature

framed views of the lakes, the centerpiece of the main vista. They also act as an exquisite line of filigree between the house, lawn, and the lakes, echoing the landscape pictures of Camille Corot.

The change of level between the plateau and the footprint of this garden could be read as a postmodernist, late-twentieth-century, American version of the British eighteenth-century ha-ha. Then, it was a ditch and retaining wall separating the garden of a country house from adjacent grazing land while giving an uninterrupted view over the open countryside beyond. Hargreaves has adapted this historical garden incident in order to create a wonderful, uninterrupted lake view.

The design and construction of the garden took two and a half years from start to finish. Hargreaves worked closely with the Daytons, the contractor, and the gardener, who now maintains the garden:

> All of the key players were involved with the project from the beginning, so no one can say, "I didn't know that." The client would ask good basic questions: "How much does it cost? Is it maintainable? Does it make sense with the house?" Pretty much questions that a major Midwestern retailer would ask, very sharp. The collaboration was an interesting discipline, for the client asked those questions throughout the process, and having the gardener in on the meetings meant we had the opinion of the man who's going to maintain it.

When asked about any constraints on those "*wonderful,* necessary and constant givens of any landscape project—good ol' Time and Money," Hargreaves comments:

> Yes, there was a constraint on time. The clients had sold their property, and they had to move into the new house by a certain date, so we had to be out by that date. We fast-tracked a couple of things, like we were building things before we had a full set of drawings and stuff like that. Money, I was never

**Above**  Small Green Stone Circle *was made in 1985 by Richard Shelton.*

**Below**  *Ellsworth Kelly's sculpture,* Untitled (Triptych), *1982, in the foreground and Richard Serra's* Garden Arc.

really given a budget, but everything was sort of vetted . . . A lot of things that were concrete were slowly turned to stone. It pushes up the cost, but they were interested in the longevity . . . So in a meeting we'd sit and say that concrete was seven dollars per foot and limestone was twenty-five dollars a foot. I'd give a recommendation, and as we got closer and closer to building, the process would tip, and the *right* decision would be made.

As for the general guidelines he followed in designing the garden, Hargreaves says that the clients wanted both a serene environment and a place to live gracefully. Then they hammered away at him for a year to make sure they got exactly what they wanted. He would propose, and the Daytons would dispose!

*Above A view from the living room out to the terrace, with Scott Burton's witty marble bench, Six Part Settee, 1984. Beyond it lies the lawn and the top of the curved retaining wall. The climax of the view is the lake, seen through a Corot-esque filigree of bare trees.*

# Daniel Urban Kiley

## A Connecticut Estate

*I find direct and simple expressions of function and site to be the most potent. In many cases, though not all, this has led me to design using classic geometries to order spaces that are related in a continuous spatial system, that indicates connections beyond itself, ultimately with the universe.*

Daniel Urban Kiley

Once, when Dan Kiley was on the point of giving a presentation, a fellow architect urged him to "go easy on the geometry because you're thought of as a neoclassicist." Kiley snapped back, "Forget the 'neo.'" This case study presents a country site set in low, rolling hills with spectacular views to the forested Taconic Range of mountains—a brilliant East Coast autumn panorama of color when the leaves of the maples turn their brilliant shades of red and yellow.

This is a case of Le Nôtre comes to New England. Alternatively, one could apply Mark Twain's *A Connecticut Yankee in King Arthur's Court.* Daniel Urban Kiley could feel very much at home as "a Vermont Yankee in King Louis XIV's Court."

In this formal design, Kiley has brought the shade of André Le Nôtre to Connecticut. Louis XIV's garden designer for Versailles would appreciate Kiley's use of the formal landscape language of geometry. Kiley acknowledges the Frenchman as a major design "ancestor."

Kiley has made a splendid classical design for the large garden of this grand American country house. Remembering back to the very beginning of the project, he said:

Upon viewing the site, my first thought was of a nice Beefeater martini with lemon twist . . . Seriously, my first visit with the client was a bit strange; time the architect was let go. I saw that the house was quite large, fourteen thousand square feet, and stained a dull brown. It rankled with the peaceful countryside of southwestern Connecticut. I said, "You know you have to paint this white?" After initial shock, the clients agreed, and the entire structure is now a pure, harmonious traditional white and sits well in the New England countryside.

**Far right** *A panorama of meadow, lake, and the glorious Taconic Mountain range seen from the formal terrace in Kiley's garden for a Connecticut estate.*

---

### GARDEN STATISTICS

**Client:** Withheld at clients' request

**Budget:** N/A

**Designer:** Office of Dan Kiley

**Area:** 600 acres

**Climate:** Zones 4–5

**Soil type:** Clay/loam

**Aspect:** South-west

**Date of completion:** 1996

**Number of gardeners:** 2

**Far right** *Snakearm by Peter Shelton stands at the far end of an allée of honey locusts.* Untitled (Triptych), *by Ellsworth Kelly, 1982, is seen in profile in the foreground of the picture.*

**Below** *David Nash's sculpture* Standing Trunk + Limb, *1988, on landforms that Hargreaves calls "elongated pyramids with isosceles construction."*

studio was opened in Cambridge, Massachusetts. Many of the company's California projects display an ability to emphasize the elemental in the landscape. At Byxbee Park, Palo Alto, the profile of landforms was taken from distant hills. The existing site was covered in trash to a depth of sixty feet. The firm solved this problem by spreading two feet of good soil sown with native grasses and wildflowers over twelve inches of impenetrable clay sealer. At Candlestick Cultural Park, South San Francisco, strong winds and their sounds were harnessed to the concrete Wind Gate. At Prospect Green, Sacramento, a flat valley was sculpted into landforms from earth ravaged by gold dredging.

George Hargreaves has designed gardens for just two private houses. The first was a stunning series of spirals and serpentines of contrasting grasses and wildflowers, set in a forest clearing of holm oaks and mesquite. The design contrasted with a large, white stucco, angular, asymmetric modernist house—Villa Zapu—on a hillside at the end of the Napa Valley in California.

The second is the subject of this case study. It is the Dayton residence, a rectilinear modernist villa in Minneapolis, Minnesota. Its setting, overlooking some of greater Minneapolis's many lakes, recalls two other International Style villas: the Farnsworth House by Mies van der Rohe outside Chicago and its Connecticut offspring, the Glass House by Philip Johnson. This building by local architect Vincent James Associates also has echoes of the Villa Savoye, designed by Le Corbusier outside Paris.

The history of this project is rooted in the Daytons' decision to leave their house at Wayzata and move into the city. The grounds of their old home

Case Studies

**Right** *The pergola on the lawn terrace is used for croquet. A jet rises from a sleek, contemporary plane of water that mirrors the sky and clouds. The rectilinear black slate block carries three inches of recycled water falling down copper-sheathed sides.*

**Below** *The serpentine retaining wall creates a plinth of formal terraces. Kiley sees this as a means of defining the house complex in relation to the surrounding sylvan landscape of the estate.*

Kiley was commissioned to deal with the fifty acres nearest the house, creating a balanced transition between this area and the untouched countryside beyond. He explained his approach to the creation of this transition in the following way:

What inspires me is to develop the undiscovered relationships between the house and the land and let these be the diagram for the landscape design. One never needs to make up a design—just go to the site with clear eyes, listen to the client's needs with an open mind, and seek the highest solution . . . it evolves!

When asked about the constraints set by the client on time or money, Kiley replied:

None. When we began the project in 1993, the client was almost as old as I was. He told me, "I don't want any green bananas." In other words, the project was to appear fully mature on installation; therefore, we selected large-girthed trees: fifteen-inch-caliper sweet chestnuts, fourteen-inch-caliper gingko, eight-foot-high hornbeam hedges, and other wonderful plants to insure that structural elements of the landscape—allées, bosques, lines of trees, and other shapes—imparted the full effect of the design immediately.

When we asked Kiley about his ideas regarding the concept of space in the project, he gave the following explanation:

The concept and treatment of space is the same for all projects . . . in terms of shaping and creating dynamic spatial volume with screens and lines of hedges and trees, groundcover, grass, water, and crushed stone panels, etc. The use of light and shadow, and seasonal effects, are essential to developing clarity of relationships. I celebrate space in the same way: integrate the existing with the new; interpret the client's program and the site's characteristics within a spatial order of unity and clarity; develop details and nuance which bring the essence of spiritual connection to the universe and beyond. I try to access the delight and mystery in daily life and in seasonal change, to be revealed in the design.

The major classical details near the house are a simple but hefty pergola, some formally set trees, lawns, and a couple of raised water features. Each water feature is one hundred feet long. Together, they form part of massive, poured-concrete retaining walls that bound the house on two sides at a height of six feet and create the perimeter of the north terrace.

The pergola has poured-concrete columns and wooden lintel crosspieces. Wisteria is planted at each of the columns. The paving under the pergola is square carnelian granite pavers set with wide grass "mortar" courses. This stone-grass design is a Kiley signature in many of his gardens. The grass between the pavers

**Above** *Kiley's early perspective sketch shows the juxtaposition of the serpentine retaining wall and rectilinear water feature.*

**Left** *Immaculately designed and installed retaining walls with the Barbara Hepworth sculpture* Two Figures, *1968, in bronze with color.*

**Above** *Formal serenity created with a few well-considered garden elements.*

makes a softer effect than closely set, mortared stones, and appears to be an extension of the lawn ground plane. Maintenance is simplified also, for the grass "mortar courses" can be mowed when the lawn is cut.

Trees are set formally in pairs, allées, bosques, and lines. A pair of *Gingko biloba* in circles of periwinkle is in the arrival court, becoming visible only after one traverses the main drive through an allée of red maples. This is the eastern side of the house, and the entry court opposite the front door is defined by a square bosque of crabapples underplanted with periwinkle and cotoneaster. A two-lane porte cochère shelters the main door; the round columns are painted black, and the roof has two triangular skylights. On the eastern side there are two lines of lindens shielding the conservatory from the setting sun.

The long retaining wall, which bounds the site on two sides, serves to focus and define the house and garden within the larger landscape. Abutting the wall are other large areas of grass, and adjacent to it is agricultural land, which merges into the rolling hills and the mountains on the horizon.

The historic precedent for massive walls used to level and retain the soil near a house can be found in both Italy and France. Huge retaining walls were designed by Michelozzo for Cosimo de Medici at the sixteenth-century Villa Medici in Fiesole. They are considered to be the first such constructions during the Italian Renaissance. In seventeenth-century France, Le

Nôtre's redesign of the gardens of Chantilly for Louis II de Bourbon, "le Grand Condé," included the construction of retaining walls for new terraces and for the gigantic grand canal.

Long rectangular canals and basins were another feature common in many French gardens of the seventeenth century. Kiley has installed his own version of the formal canal in this garden. It consists of two rectangular granite water features, set at a right angle and retained by the rampart. A very shallow depth of water falls down over three narrow steps on the face of the granite, making three long, gentle waterfalls. The smooth water on the surface of the sixty dark granite rectangles mirrors the changing sky. At the angle where two "canal" shapes meet, Kiley has designed a square pool from which shoots a tall and vigorous jet that he calls a "roiling fountain." The jet creates a dramatic end stop. The fountain by the house also feeds a woodland runnel that cascades down the western slope through a grove of birch and ferns. This runnel spills into a constructed bog, ringed with black spruce and swamp azalea, sited at one end of the pond. Discussing the versatility of the water used in the garden, Kiley explained:

> Water is used in several forms to express varied character. Each interpretation of water expresses a specific purpose—cool and elegant on the terrace, rich, fragrant, and cloistered in the bog; bubbling and playful as the fountain which is viewed from

**Right** *Nighttime in this Connecticut landscape. The up-lit trees add mystery to the meadow and mountain vista on a summer evening.*

within the library and bar of the house.

In his use of water, Kiley shows the mature mastery of his art. If the rectangular water features had been conventional pools, they would need high maintenance, with algae, leaves, and other detritus for the gardeners to remove. Here they must deal only with the narrow pool at the base of the raised rectangle of granite.

Daniel Urban Kiley is the most respected landscape architect in the United States. His career has spanned sixty years. In 1997 he was awarded the National Medal of Art for distinguished service to landscape architecture. Over the decades he has designed some 1,500 private and public gardens, often in collaboration with some of this century's leading firms of American architects: Skidmore, Owings & Merrill, Roche and Dinkeloo, Louis Kahn, Philip Johnson, I. M. Pei, and Eero Saarinen. Many of his designs have become twentieth-century landmarks. As Pei says:

> Kiley is the best. He belongs to that tradition
> of, let's say, the big thinkers in the field. He is not
> just limited to doing a small house and garden.
> He also has tremendous scope and breadth in
> his thinking about landscape. He treats
> landscape with grand gestures.

Kiley/Pei projects have included Fountain Place, Dallas, Texas; the John F. Kennedy Library, Dorchester, Massachusetts; and the East Wing of the National

Gallery, Washington, D.C. In 1999, Kiley is eighty-six years old, and he is working again with Pei and Mario Bellini on an eight-acre site in Kyoto, Japan. Over the whole site he has designed a grid of twenty-eight-foot squares of gravel, moss, and water across which diagonals of raised, mounded shapes intervene. Seeing the plan at his studio in the woods near Charlotte, Vermont, we said that we thought he must have been inspired by an intricate Japanese silk kimono or the *obi* of a court lady from medieval Japan. He laughed and replied that it was a garden and nothing more. But, we think he was interested by the comparison.

Studying the designs of Dan Kiley and other leading classicists, we have been struck by the wonderful congruence or "fit" between International Style architecture and the geometry of the ancient formal style and its variations through the history of garden design. As Dan Kiley, America's master landscape architect, says: "Landscape is not mere adornment but an integral part of the disposition of space, plane, line, and structure with which it is associated."

**Above** *Kiley's master plan, which clearly shows the relationship of the square and rectilinear elements of the house and adjacent gardens to the gentle land contours, lake, and wilder elements of the landscape. As Kiley says, "The challenge was to develop an effective exterior sequence which would respond appropriately to its physical and historical setting."*

### Desert Breath, El Ghouna, Egypt

*The conical volume is a familiar form in the language of the desert. It becomes a point of reference in the endless procession of horizons. As we create conical volumes that are precise geometrical forms, their origin moves into the realm of the mysterious . . . the moment they are completed, they become an instrument to measure the passage of time.*

D.A.ST.

*Far right An aerial view of the site-generated landscape project Desert Breath, which is located near the Red Sea in Egypt.*

D.A.ST. consists of three artists: Danae Stratou, sculptor; Alexandra Stratou, industrial designer; and Stella Constantinides, architect. The group was formed in the spring of 1995 to collaborate on an installation in the desert. They envisioned a site-specific work on such a scale that it could be fully experienced only on foot. It takes forty minutes to walk around the finished structure.

In June 1995, they went to Egypt in search of a suitable site. They settled upon a large expanse of desert six hours south of Cairo. It lies between the coast of the Red Sea and a ridge called the Eastern Mountains. Here, in an atmosphere of great excitement and enthusiasm, they reached an agreement about the concept for the project, Desert Breath.

When they returned to their homes on the Greek island of Paros, one of the windiest places in the Mediterranean, they spent the rest of the summer testing their concept using sand models and computer-generated sketches. In September their proposal was approved by Samih Sawiris, the president of Orascom, a construction and development company based in Cairo. Sawiris and his enthusiasm proved to be fundamental to the eventual success of the project.

Until September 1996, D.A.ST. worked with architects, engineers, mathematicians, and geologists on final detailing. The team returned to the site several times to discuss exact site selection and construction methods.

The construction of Desert Breath began in June 1996 and was complete nine months later. The finished project covers an area of more than a million square feet and has a total diameter of 1,460 feet, resulting in the displacement of 280,000 cubic feet of sand. The two interlocking logarithmic

**GARDEN STATISTICS**

**Client:** Samih Sawiris, Orascom Construction PTD, Cairo

**Designer:** D.A.ST.

**Area:** 1,076,426 square feet

**Climate:** Desert

**Soil type:** Sand

**Aspect:** West

**Date of completion:** 1997

spirals consist of 178 cones. They have a single center with a phase difference of 180 degrees in the same direction of rotation. One spiral is made from "positive" cones, rising above the desert grade. The other is made from "negative" cones, which were excavated below grade. The positive cones are formed from the sand that was displaced to make the negative ones. They range in height from twenty inches to twelve feet.

The concept of the cone shapes was first inspired by piles of sand spoil that had resulted from road building in the area. D.A.ST. noticed that when the wind-blown sand collected at the feet of desert plants, it created a cone shape around the base. This natural combination of sand and wind inspired the team to create cone shapes themselves.

The correct compaction of the sand used to construct both the positive and negative cones was crucial. It was achieved through a combination of manual labor and earthmoving equipment. Initially, D.A.ST. thought that the cones could be dug and compacted at random. However, it soon became clear that they had to be worked on as a series. The team gives full credit to the skills of their digger driver, Ahmed. His control of the machine was such that he was able to judge the correct depth of each negative

*Below* The beginning of one of the two interlocking sand-cone spirals inspired by the cones of sand deposited on the stems of indigenous plants by the action of the wind.

cone by eye. In order to make the positive cones, it was crucial to calculate the angle of deposition. This is the critical point of mass at which the sand falls away, and getting it wrong would ruin the cone shape.

Water is another major element of the design. The lack of water in the desert and a view of the Red Sea inspired the notion of a circular pool. It is a beaten-earth concavity with a diameter of one hundred feet. The center of the pool was filled with a giant cone calculated to have only its tip above the finished water level. When the pool is filled to the brim, the protruding cone becomes the central incident of the design and can be read as a small island on the horizon. It is the mathematical starting point of the double spiral cones.

It was crucial to D.A.ST. that all of the elements of the design should be finished at the same time. They wanted the moment of completion to be "time zero", before the forces of nature began to work their inevitable transformation.

Desert Breath represents an important moment for land art in the 1990s. As with the projects of the 1960s and 1970s, documentation will be crucial. The team has returned frequently to the site in 1998 and

**Left** *While constructing the double spiral cones, the D.A.ST. team found that the positive and negative cones had to be dug in height and depth sequence: from the largest to the smallest.*

1999, using videos and photographs to record the gradual changes wrought on Desert Breath, the "harmonic cohabitation of the precision of human geometry with that of nature."

The choice of location was vital to the concept of this project. The desolate site meant that D.A.ST.'s "marks" should remain undisturbed by humankind. They will be "disturbed," however, by that most pervasive of natural elements of the desert, the wind. The mobility of the sand controlled by the wind will eventually change, if not obliterate, the cones. This is yet another perfect example of the universe's principle of construction and destruction.

D.A.ST. Art Team says of its fantastic land creation: The project is rooted in our common desire to work in the desert. The lack of objects in the surrounding area renders one unable to rely on customary means in order to determine scale, space, distance, and orientation, so that these acquired senses have to be relearned based on experience with earth (gravity), sky (motion), light (change), water (level). Simultaneously, one experiences a feeling of isolation and completeness. One can feel time go by, yet provide no resistance. The vastness of the horizon becomes the only visual reference to equilibrium.

**Below** *Walking the spiral pathway. D.A.ST. has documented the inevitable changes to Desert Breath since its construction using photos and videos.*

The collaborating designers are Kathryn
Gustafson, Neil Porter, and John Lyall.
They say, "Crystal Palace Park gives an
overwhelming feeling of being a lost place, a past
dream with vestiges that seem unconnected to
today's world." The new park would create a
series of brilliant cross-references between past
and present. There would be a number of
different gardens and an axis of glasshouses

# The New Crystal Palace Park Project, London

relating to Joseph Paxton's original terraces. The
first phase has received partial funding to cover
the restoration element of the project.

*This was the winning entry for the children's park*

*competition in 1990–1991. It was created by the*

*design team of the late Alexei Meshcherjakov and*

## Park Detski  Moscow, Meshcherjakov & Tolkachev

*Oleg Tolkachev, trained in the landscape course*

*of Professor Kraskov at the Moscow Architecture*

*Institute. It is one of many theme park projects*

*designed in Russia after Kruschev's visit to*

*Disneyland, Los Angeles, in 1959. Russian*

*mysticism, historicism and a strong eighteenth-*

*century formal grid are all elements of the*

*design. Most Russian landscape architects*

*present their work as paintings like this,*

*rather than in drawing form.*

On the former site of the medieval walls of

the city and its Friesentor (an important city

gate), Foster & Partners, London, has designed

# Gerling-Ring, Cologne Desvigne & Dalnoky

a mixed-use project of offices, apartments, and

retail units. The landscape improvements, or

"greening," of the five internal open spaces and

the tops of the flat roofs have been designed by

Desvigne & Dalnoky, Paris. There are large-scale

water features in various conformations: pools—

including plinths for sculpture—a large terrace,

canals, and water walls. There are also areas of

dense plantings of azaleas and rhododendrons,

which will all contrast with the rectilinear

architecture.

*An eight-acre development in Kyoto, including*

*an office, hotel, commercial, and cultural*

*complex, involves the architects I. M. Pei*

# Mid-Kyoto Master Plan Daniel Urban Kiley

*and Mario Bellini. Kiley's master plan, in three*

*layers, is a reinterpretation of Japanese gardens*

*and culture. The primary layer is a twenty-five-*

*foot square grid across the site. Two walkway*

*systems follow the grid lines, reinforced by lines of*

*moss and groundcover. Between the grid lines are*

*alternating panels of grass and clipped azaleas,*

*with a groundcover of bulbs and water. The*

*second layer is created by quartets of trees*

*planted in grid panels. The third layer, placed*

*across the grid, is serpentine mounds of moss,*

*azaleas, and other plantings.*

A Danish schools-of-the-future competition was
won by Stig L. Andersson, a leading Danish
landscape architect. The school is part of a

## The Trekroner School, Copenhagen Stig L. Andersson

new-town project. Andersson's view of the
landscape is contextual and flexible. The
schoolyard will be replaced by a school garden.
An asphalt basin lake can be emptied for roller-
blading and skateboarding; artificial rock is
provided for climbing; and there are areas for
flower and vegetable gardens.

*Le Meuble Qui Pousse (The Growing Building),*

*Montpelier, by Edouard François and Associates,*

*was a winner of Millennium 2000, France,*

## Le Meuble Qui Pousse, Montpelier Edouard François & Associates

*Projects for Architecture. Sited on the River Lez*

*outside Montpelier, Edouard François's building is*

*green and growing. It is in a grove of mature*

*plane trees. The roofless rooms on stilts are*

*among the branches. Gabion stone walls and a*

*second skin of Turkish volcanic stone create soil*

*pockets for drought-resistant succulent plants. The*

*entire facade was sprayed with water, pig*

*manure, and seeds. This visionary, verdant seven-*

*story apartment building cost 22 million francs;*

*purchasers lined up to buy.*

*This public park is on the River Nervión, adjacent*

*to Frank Gehry's Guggenheim Museum. John*

*Beardsley describes Diana Balmori's work in the*

## Abandoibarra Park, Bilbao Balmori Associates

*following way: "[She] has worked to reveal as*

*many of the natural and cultural layers as possible*

*that are evident in a site, encompassing ecology,*

*history, the demographics of adjacent*

*communities, and the social uses of the landscape.*

*She has made herself attentive to the various*

*possibilities for environmental remediation, from*

*the restoration of derelict urban landscapes to the*

*repair of damaged ecosystems."*

*Adriaan Geuze established his Rotterdam-based office in 1987. The practice is named for the strong wind that sweeps across the Netherlands'*

## 1:00 PM Square, New York West 8 and Adriaan Geuze

*polder. The designs are site generated and contextual. Geuze says, "We love popular culture, we love the dock culture, the technical effects, we love the esthetics of non-design." 1:00 PM Square is a design for Madison Square in the heart of Manhattan. Giant topiary constructions would humanize this area of the city's grid; instead of offering only a few trees, the site would become a "green village."*

# Afterword

A received prevailing attitude in the landscape architecture profession over the past twenty years or so turns on the view that it is without a sufficient body of critical writings, that it is without models, that it has no focused direction, and, finally, that twentieth-century landscape design lacks art. Art in the garden and landscape does emerge, but not because some landscape designers and architects proclaim self-consciously about art and question endlessly whether or not theirs or a very few practitioners' work is art. George Hargreaves explains another view:

> I dislike the drive toward everything to do with metaphors and art meanings. Well, you know, a row of trees being simply a row of trees, they don't have to represent the essence of life or some grounding in nineteenth-century or twentieth-century thought, they can simply be a row of trees. You can then bring whatever interpretation you want to bring to it, from nothing, to "I like it," and the row of trees can stand simply as elements. They don't have to be skewed into metaphors, they don't have to have a purpose as, or be in something else, they can simply be themselves, a row of trees; it has taken me twenty years to get to that.

Some gardens and landscapes can be called art or have fulfilled an aspiration toward art, for they are uniquely expressive, or the projects have solved problems of human activity both usefully and aesthetically within the reality of a site, or perhaps they just "are," in some way to enough people, exquisite or beautiful. Maybe, they emerge only from landscape designers who have what Philip Johnson called in a lecture "the fire in the belly," that mysterious source of creative energy and vision.

Some garden and landscape designs of the twentieth century do have that vision, we feel, and "sing" to us. The landscapes we would define as art are Dan Kiley's Miller Garden, Isamu Noguchi's California Scenario, George Hargreaves's Villa Zapu, Charles Jencks's Garden of Cosmic Speculation, and Robert Irwin's Lower Central Garden at the Getty Center.

A. A. Gill, one of Britain's most perceptive and controversial critics, offered this opinion of contemporary art when reviewing a recent television series.

> The trajectory of modern art is plainly all downhill. It is a medium in steady, precipitous decline, running on empty. The conclusion is inescapable; art has painted itself into a box of its own devising, from where it has no vision or talent or the will to find a response to the real world.

Gill's view could be called extreme, and even blinkered, but we do think the work of the landscape architects and designers shown in this book is evidence of "a response to the real world," as opposed to some of the accepted leading-edge art of the past ten years in Britain: a pharmacy cabinet filled with boxes of medicines, a fried egg and sausage on a pine table, a small canvas tent inside of which are embroidered the many names of the conceptual craftperson's lovers. These were exhibited in the Sensation exhibition at the Royal Academy, London, 1998.

Is contemporary art really without models and focus, other than those approved by the mutually self-interested group of curators, collectors, dealers, and critics, all of whom need, in some way, to find and promote ever newer products for their consumers? As opposed to another accepted view that many landscape architects and designers hold about their work—that it is always following other major design, art, and cultural activities—we think there are signs that quite the opposite is happening.

In fact, it seems to us that over the past twenty years, landscape and garden design has been, in certain aspects of thinking and practice, leading, not following, the other arts in this difficult and complicated cultural assessment. Landscape and garden design appear now to have more direction and focus than current contemporary art. Designs for the

landscape embody a connectedness, a concern with an actuality—the land we walk on, where we live, work, and play—all materialized through a responsiveness to the real world.

Several of the case studies, along with some of the future designs in the final section, are inspired by the philosophy of the site generated or contextual. This approach is the advance in the late twentieth century on all of the past, for these designs can reflect directly the context of our lives within contemporary culture.

**This page and opposite** Tree Lung of the Earth by D.A.ST. Art Team. The viewer walks into a large, dark room with the scent of earth-covered floor and moist air. Unifying the elements are the sounds: forest mixed with a breathing accentuated by a single drop on an amplified drum. In the center is a large volume of twenty by twenty by ten feet. Video images shot in real time over one day are projected in real time on the high wall. Sun filtering through tree and plant movement creates a suspension of time. Landscape into art? Art into landscape?

# Index

*Page numbers in italics refer to illustrations.*

# Bibliography

Abington Art Center Sculpture Garden. *Winifred Lutz, A Reclamation Garden 1992–1993*. USA: Abington Art Center Publication,1996.

Abington Art Center Sculpture Garden. *Winifred Lutz, A Reclamation Garden 1993–1995*. USA: Abington Art Center Publication,1996.

Abington Art Center. *The Garden Matrix*. USA: Abington Art Center Publication, 1996. (Program to support the creation and installation for outdoor sculpture.)

Adams, William Howard. *Denatured Visions: Landscape and Culture in the Twentieth Century*. USA: Museum of Modern Art, 1991.

Adams, William Howard. *Roberto Burle Marx, The Unnatural Art of the Garden*. USA: Museum of Modern Art, 1991.

Anderton, Frances. "Avant-Gardens." *Architectural Review*, September 1989. (Peter Walker and Martha Schwartz)

Arriola, Andreu, Adriaan Geuze, Steen Hoyer, Bernard Huet, Peter Latz, David Louwerse, Norfried Pohl, and Clemens Steenbergen. *Modern Park Design, Recent Trends*. Holland: Thoth Publishers, 1995 (Second Edition).

Atkins, Robert. *Art Speak*. USA: Abbeville Press, 1990.

Atkins, Robert. *Art Spoke*. USA: Abbeville Press, 1993.

Baljon, Lodewijk. *Designing Parks*. U.K.: Garden Art Press, 1992.

Barnett, Rod. "Rod Barnett Examines a Contemporary Landscape and the Politics of Place." New Zealand: *Landscape New Zealand*, Nov/Dec 1997. (Quay Park, Ted Smyth design)

Beardsley, John. *Earthworks and Beyond. Contemporary Art in the Landscape*. USA: Abbeville Press, 1998 (Third Edition).

Beardsley, John. "Making Waves." USA: *Landscape Architecture*, March 1998. (Charles Jencks's Garden)

Begley, Adam. "Secret Garden." USA: *Connoisseur*, April 1991. (Millbrook Garden)

Bennett, Paul. "Big Ideas Down Under." USA: *Landscape Architecture*, February 1999. (George Hargreaves's Olympic Park in Sydney).

Brand, Jan, Catelijne de Muynck and Jouke Kleerebezem. *Allocations: Art for a Natural and Artificial Environment*. The Hague-Zoetermeer, Holland: Floriade Foundation, 1992.

Caploe, David. "The Pros and Cons of Miami Style." USA: *New Miami*, July 1990. (Raymond Jungles and Debra Lynn Yates).

Celan, Paul. *Selected Poems*. USA: Penguin Books,1996.

Cerver, Francisco Asensio. *World of Environmental Design: Landscape Art*. Barcelona: Arco,1995.

Cerver, Francisco Asensio. *World of Environmental Design: Landscape of Recreation II (Amusement Parks)*. Barcelona: Arco, 1994.

Compton, Tania. "Gardening à la Mode." U.K.: *House & Garden*, April 1998. (Chanel Garden at Chelsea Flower Show).

Corbett, Sue. "Large but Perfectly Formed." U.K.: *Country Life*, January 28, 1999. (Modern sculptors working in gardens).

D.A.ST. Art Team. *Desert Breath*. Athens, Greece: D.A.ST. Art Team, 1997.

Deitz, Paula. "Fearless Gardening." USA: *House Beautiful*, May, 1995. (LongHouse, Jack Lenor Larsen).

Deitz, Paula. "Recultivating the Tuileries." USA: *Design Quarterly*, Spring, 1992. (Jacques Wirtz and Peter Wirtz).

Domaine de Kerguehennec. *Catalogue of Site Specific Sculpture Collection*. Brittany, France.

Don, Montagu. "Chanel's Natural Look." U.K.: *Observer Life*, May 31, 1998. (Chanel's Chelsea Flower Show Garden).

Ducas, Jane. "Come into the Garden, Karl." U.K.: *Saturday Telegraph Magazine, May 23, 1998*. (Chanel Chelsea Flower Show Garden).

Eckbo, Garrett. "Is Landscape Architecture?". USA: *Landscape Architecture*, May 1983.

Eckbo, Garrett. "Garrett Eckbo: Philosophy of Landscape." Tokyo, Japan: *Process: Architecture*, 90 (1990).

Edwards, J.G. "The Constancy of Change." Japan: *Mainichi Daily News*, December 10, 1987. (Arata Isozaki).

Edwards, Lawrence. *The Vortex of Life*. U.K.: Floris Books, 1993.

Elle Decoration. "Le Monde Etrange de Monsieur Jencks." France: *Elle Decoration*, No.58, October 1995. (The lifestyle of Charles Jencks).

Emmet, Alan. "How Green is His Valley." USA: *House & Garden*, March, 1999. (Robert Irwin Design of Lower Central Garden at Getty Center, Los Angeles).

Evans, Barrie. "The Well-Tempered Environment." U.K.: *The Architects' Journal*, July 27, 1994. (Ian Ritchie Architects' design for a park building in the Dordogne).

Everdell, William R. *The First Moderns*. USA: The University of Chicago Press, 1997.

Filler, Martin. "The Recent Work of Arata Isozaki: Part I." USA: *Architectural Record*, October 1983. (Business Design Engineering, a McGraw-Hill Publication).

Finch, Paul. "Combining Artifice and Nature in the Dordogne." U.K.: *The Architects' Journal*, November 9, 1995. (Ian Ritchie's design for a park building in the Dordogne).

Flanagan, Barbara. "A Healing Place in the Sun." USA: *The New York Times*, January 15, 1998. (Topher Delaney).

Futagawa, Yoshio. *Bernard Tschumi. GA Document Extra 10*. Japan: A.D.A. EDITA, Tokyo, 1997.

Gerlach-Spriggs, Nancy, Richard Enoch Kaufman and Sam Bass Warner, Jr. *Restorative Gardens: The Healing Landscape*. New Haven & London: Yale University Press, 1998.

Gill, A.A. "Corset Makes Sense." UK: *The Sunday Times, (Culture)*, June 13, 1999. (TV Programme Review: "What is Modern Art?").

Gillette, Jane Brown. "Kiley Revisited." USA: *Landscape Architecture*, August, 1998.

Gillette, Jane Brown. "Pure Design, Pure Image." USA: *Landscape Architecture*, October, 1998. (The Dayton Garden designed by George Hargreaves).

Glancey, Jonathan. "The Hole in the Heart." U.K.: *The Guardian*, January 27, 1999. (Daniel Libeskind's Jewish Museum, Berlin).

Goldsworthy, Andy. *Touching North*. UK: Fabian Carlsson, Graeme Murray, 1989.

Goldsworthy, Andy. *Stone*. U.K.: Viking, 1994.

Goodwin, Stephen. "Garden Grows in Fertile Soil of Science and the Senses." UK: *The Independent*, November 17, 1997. (Charles Jencks's garden).

Grant, Bill and Paul Harris (editors). *Natural Order. Visual Arts & Crafts in Grizedale Forest Park*. U.K.: The Grizedale Society, 1996.

Greenberg, Stephen. "Libeskindbau Leads Where Other Museums Should Follow." UK: *The Architect's Journal*, February 28, 1999. (New Jewish Museum in Berlin).

Griswold, Mac. "A History of the Sanctuary Garden." USA: *Design Quarterly 169*, Summer 1996.

Griswold, Mac. "Brooding Forest As Artist's Medium." USA: *The New York Times*, November 20, 1997. (Reclamation Garden at Abington Art Center).

Griswold, Mac. "The Therapeutic Garden." USA: *Landscape Architecture*, 1996. (Healing Garden at Wellesley, MA.).

Hammerslough, Jane. "The Children's Garden" USA: *Garden Design*, June/July, 1997. (Healing Garden at Wellesley, MA.)

Heizer, Michael. *Germano Celant*. Italy: Fondazione Prada, 1997.

Hirsch, Jeffrey. *Seeing the Getty Gardens*. 1998. (Getty Center, Los Angeles).

Hoffman, E. T. A. *The Life and Opinions of the Tomcat Murr*. UK: Penguin Books, 1999. (Hoffman Anthology)

Holden, Robert. *International Landscape Design*. U.K.: Laurence King Publishing, 1996.

*Hortus Third: A Concise Dictionary of Plants Cultivated in the United States and Canada*. USA: Macmillan Publishing, 1976

Hughes, Robert. *The Shock of the New*. U.K.: Thames and Hudson, 1991.

*The Hutchinson Encyclopedia (New 8th Edition)*. UK: Century Hutchinson Ltd, 1988.

Imbert, Dorothee. *The Modernist Garden in France*. USA: Yale University Press, 1993.

International Kunstcentrum deSingel. *The Landscape, Four International Landscape Designers (Hargreaves Associates, Desvigne & Dalnoky, West 8 Landscape Architects, Torres & Lapeña)*. (Museum Catalogue). Holland: deSingel, 1995.

Iovine, Julie V. "Sermon on the Mound" USA: *The New York Times Magazine*, February 4, 1996. (Charles Jencks's Garden).

Iovine, Julie V. "Fountain Fantasies, From Cascades to Curbs." USA: *The New York Times*, June 11, 1998. (Dan Kiley and Water Features).

Irwin, Robert. *Retrospective Exhibition: 1993*. Catalogue. Museum of Contemporary Art, Los Angeles & Rizzoli International Publications, New York, 1993.

Jaffe, Matthew. "Acropolis Now." US: *Sunset*, January 1998. (The $1-billion Getty Center).

Jellicoe, Geoffrey and Susan, Patrick Goode and Michael Lancaster. *The Oxford Companion to Gardens*. UK: Oxford University Press, 1986.

Jencks, Charles. "New Science—New Architecture." Japan: *A+U*, June 1995. (Charles Jencks's Philosophy).

Johnson, Jory. "Martha Schwartz's "Splice Garden": A Warning to a Brave New World." USA: *Landscape Architecture*, August 7, 1988.

Karson, Robin. "Conversation with Kiley" USA: *Landscape Architecture*, December, 1988.

Karson, Robin. *Fletcher Steele, Landscape Architect, an account of a garden maker's life*. USA: Abrams, 1989.

Kaster, Jeffrey, and Brian Wallis. *Land and Environmental Art*. U.K.: Phaidon, 1998.

Kaufman, Ann. "A New Expression of Japan Emerges Through a Collection of Western Themes." (Isozaki's Civic Center in Tsukuba). Japan: *Far Eastern Economic Review*, May 31, 1984.

Kearton, Diane, (Editor). *Art & the Garden*. U.K.: Academy Group Ltd., 1997.

*Dan Kiley: Landscape Design II – in Step with Nature. Process: Architecture, No. 108*. Japan: 1993.

Kiley, Dan and Jane Amidon. *Dan Kiley in His Own Words*. U.K.: Thames & Hudson, 1999.

Kindt, Sven and Eric Messerschmidt. *The Danish Wave*. Exhibition Catalogue. Copenhagen: The Danish Center for Architecture, 1998.

Klein, Marjorie. "Fahkahatchee Kid." USA: *Home & Garden*, February 1988. (Visualist Raymond Jungles designs a sub-tropical dream).

Lacey, Stephen. Article on the Ton ter Linden garden, Holland. U.K.: *Daily Telegraph*, July 13, 1996.

Lacey, Stephen. "How Wirtz Proved to Be the Best." U.K.: *Weekend Telegraph*, June 6, 1992.

Landecker, Heidi, (Editor). *Martha Schwartz: Transfiguration of the Commonplace*. USA: Spacemaker Press, 1997.

Lane Fox, Robin. "Weather Puts the Heat on Chelsea." U.K.: *Financial Times, Weekend May 23/24, 1998* (Chelsea Flower Show).

Larsen, Jack Lenor. *A Weaver's Memoir*. USA: Harry N. Abrams, Inc., 1998.

Leccese, Michael. "Nature meets Nurture." USA: *Landscape Architecture*. January 1995.

Leviseur, Elsa. "Hargreaves Weaves." USA: *The Architectural Review*.

Levy, Leah. *Kathryn Gustafson, Sculpting the Land*. USA: Spacemaker Press, 1998.

Libeskind, Daniel and Helene Binet. *Jewish Museum, Berlin*. Germany: G + B Arts International, 1999.

Lloyd, Christopher. "In My Garden." U.K.: *Country Life*, December 18/25, 1997. (Charles Jencks's garden).

Logan, William Bryant. "Making the Stones Dance."USA: *Garden Design*, December 1994/January 1995.

(Innisfree Garden).

Lowry, Suzanne. "The Unknown Garden Guru." (Gardens Created by Jacques Wirtz). U.K.: *Telegraph Magazine*, February 4, 1995.

Lund, Annemarie. *Abstract & Book for 36th World Congress of the International Federation of Landscape Architects*. Copenhagen: Danish Architectural Press, June 1999.

Lund, Annemarie. *A Guide to Danish Landscape Architecture: 1000 –1996*. Copenhagen: Arkitektens Forlag, 1997.

Mariage, Thierry. *The World of André Le Nôtre*. USA: University of Pennsylvania Press, 1990.

Marton, Deborah. "History Moved Forward." USA: *Landscape Architecture*, January, 1999. (Gantry Plaza, designed by Thomas Balsley).

McCormick, Kathleen. "Realm of the Senses." USA: *Landscape Architecture*, January 1995.

Melloan, Joan. "A Belgian Shows the French How It's Done." U.K.: *The Bulletin*, August 8, 1991. (Jacques Wirtz's Work at The Tuilieries).

Merser, Cheryl. "Lake Water Lapping." USA: *Preservation*, November/December 1997. (Innisfree Garden).

McGeorge, Pamela. "An Artist as Landscaper." New Zealand: *NZ Gardener*, May 1998. (Ted Smyth).

Miyake, Riichie. "The Afterimage of Ruins." Tokyo: *The Japan Architect, No.* 8703. (Arata Isozaki).

Muschamp, Herbert. "Where Iron Gives Way to Beauty and Games." USA: *The New York Times*, December 13, 1998. (Gantry Plaza State Park, designed by Thomas Balsley).

Needleman, Deborah. "Shadow and Act." USA: *House and Garden*, March 1999. (Dan Kiley Garden in Connecticut).

Needleman, Deborah. "Recycled Memories." USA: *House & Garden*, March 1999. (Andrew Cao's Garden).

Owen, Jane. "Unearthing the Seeds of Chaos Theory." (Charles Jencks's Garden) U.K.: *The Times Weekend*, Saturday December 6, 1997.

Owen, Jane. "Twists and Turns." (Charles Jencks's Garden). U.K.: *The Garden*, May 1998.

P/A Profile. "Peter Walker and Martha Schwartz." USA: *Progressive Architecture*, July, 1989.

P/A Profile. "Hargreaves Associates." USA: *Progressive Architecture*, July, 1989.

Papier, Deborah. "Avant Gardeners." USA: *Avenue*, June/July, 1990. (Revolution in landscape design and the Avant-gardeners).

Pearson, Dan. "The Healing Garden." U.K.: *Gardens Illustrated*, August/September, 1998. (San Diego Children's Hospital Healing Garden, designed by Topher Delaney).

Pelle, Marie-Paule. "Zen a Madrid." Paris: *Vogue Decoration*, Edition Internationale No.10, May 1987. (Fernando Caruncho Garden).

Pegg, John. "Martha Schwartz: Learning to Build Big Art." U.K.: *Landscape Design Extra*, March, 1998.

Perlman, Heidi B. "When Helping Children, Therapist Says Nature is the Key", *Townsman*, USA: Wellesley, MA., 1996

Pigeat, Jean-Paul. "Les Jardins du Philosophie." France: *Vogue Decoration*, Paris: Edition Internationale No.38, June/July 1992. (Fernando Caruncho Gardens).

Pigeat, Jean-Paul. *Festival de Jardins*. France: Editions du Chene – Hachette Livre, 1995.

Pollak, Sally. "The Natural." USA: *The Burlington Free Press*, Sunday, November 30, 1997. (Daniel Urban Kiley).

Popham, Peter. "Teaching the Japanese to Relax." U.K.: *Blueprint*, May, 1988. (Interview with Arata Isozaki).

Popham, Peter. "Dreams of Rome." Japan: *Mainichi Daily News*, July 18, 1983. (Tsukuba "New Town").

Powers, Alan. "Figures in the Garden." U.K.: *Country Life*, January 14, 1999. (Modern Art in Public Parks).

Randall-Page, Peter. *Boulders and Banners*. UK: Exhibition Catalogue, Reed's Wharf Gallery, London SE1, London: 1995.

Raver, Anne. "In Mystical Innisfree." USA: *The New York Times*, September 1, 1994.

Raver, Anne. "When Hope Falters, Balm for the Soul." USA: *The New York Times*, December 29, 1994. (Healing Gardens).

Read, Emily. "Green Peace." USA: *American Vogue*, August, 1997. (Fernando Caruncho Gardens).

Reed, Douglas P. "The Therapeutic Garden: An Environment of Sensory and Symbolic Experiences." USA: *Art New England*, August/September, 1995.

Richardson, Martin. "A Sense of Hard Reality in an Empty Landscape." U.K.: *The Architects' Journal*, November 9, 1995. (Rotterdam Practice, West 8).

Richardson, Tim. "Editor's Manifesto." *New Eden, The Contemporary Garden Magazine*, U.K.: May/June 1999.

Richardson, Tim. "How to Garden in a Jumping Universe." U.K.: *Country Life*, October 23, 1997. (Charles Jencks's Garden).

Rodriguez, Alicia. "Celestial Connections." USA: *Landscape Architecture*, April 1998. (Rios Associates' Design at Satellite Garden, Long Beach).

Rodriguez, Sol. "Paisajes y Piscinas." Spain: *Casa & Estilo*, Ano ll, No.8.

Schama, Simon. *Landscape and Memory*. USA: Knopf & Co., 1995. (Raymond Jungles and Debra Yates).

Schneider, Bernard. *Daniel Libeskind Jewish Museum Berlin, Between the Lines*. Germany: Prestel Verlag, 1999.

Scully, Vincent. *Architecture the Natural and the Manmade*. USA: St Martin's Press, 1991.

Shields, Hatsy. "Artfully Tropical." USA: *House Beautiful*, February, 1997. (Raymond Jungles and Debra Yates).

Shopland, Alice. "Downtown Space Place." New Zealand: *NZ Herald*, December 3, 1997. (Ted Smyth's Quay Park Design).

Shrady, Nicholas. "Landscapes in Spain." USA: *Architectural Digest*, March 1998. (Fernando Caruncho Design at Mas de les Voltes).

Sitwell, Sacheverell, Osbert Sitwell, Sir George Sitwell, and Reresby Sitwell. *Hortus Sitwellianus*. USA:

Michael Russell (Publishing), 1984.

Smithson, Robert. *The Collected Writings*. (Editor: Jack Flan). Berkeley & Los Angeles: University of California Press,1996.

Spens, Michael. "Berlin Phoenix." U.K.: *Architectural Review.* February, 1999. (Daniel Libeskind Jewish Museum in Berlin).

Spens, Michael. *Landscape Transformed*. U.K.: Academy Editions, 1996.

Spirn, Anne Whiston. *The Language of Landscape*. USA: Yale University Press, 1998.

Steadman, Todd A. "Touch of Burle Marx." USA: *Landscape Architecture*, October, 1992. (Raymond Jungles' garden in Coconut Grove).

Stevens, Margaret. "Life in Fast-Forward Reverse. " USA: *Landscape Architecture,* January 1995.

Stewart, Ian. *Life's Other Secret*. U.K.: Allen Lane, The Penguin Press, 1998.

Stichting Rotterdam-Maaskant Foundation. *Adriaan Geuze/West 8.* Holland: 1995.

Stocker, Carol. "Journey into the Spirit." USA: *The Boston Globe,* October 10, 1996. (Innisfree).

Strong, Sir Roy and Julia Trevelyan Oman. *A Celebration of Gardens*. UK: HarperCollins, 1991.

Stuart-Smith, Tom. "Le Bosquet de Chanel: Camellias at the Chelsea Flower Show." UK: *International Camellia Journal.* No. 30, 1998.

Stungo, Naomi. "Germany Recalling." U.K.: *The Observer Review,* January 24, 1999. (Daniel Libeskind's New Jewish Museum).

Swaffield, Simon. "A Thoroughly Modern Man." USA: *Harvard Design Magazine,* Summer, 1998. (Ted Smyth).

Taylor, Patrick. "Visions of a Flemish Master." U.K.: *The Sunday Telegraph Magazine,* November 15, 1998. (Jacques Wirtz).

Taylor, Patrick. "Good in Beds." U.K.: *The World of Interiors,* April 1993. (Ton ter Linden).

Thacker, Christopher. *The History of Gardens*. U.K.: Croom Helm Ltd. Publishers, 1979.

Thomas, R.S. *Selected Poems: 1946–68.* U.K.: Bloodaxe Publishing, 1992.

Thompson, D'Arcy. *On Growth and Form*. U.K.: Cambridge University Press, 1961.

Thompson, Elspeth. "High Society." U.K.: *The Times Magazine,* August 22, 1998. (Tom Stuart-Smith, Garden Designer).

Tilberghien, Gilles A. *Land Art*. USA: Princeton Architectural Press, 1993.

Treib, Marc. "Fragments on a Void, Tsukuba Center." USA: *Landscape Architecture,* July/August, 1985. (Plaza designed by Arata Isozaki).

Treib, Marc, *Modern Landscape Architecture: A Critical Review.* USA: The MIT Press, 1998 (third printing).

Treib, Marc and Dorothee Imbert. *Garrett Eckbo: Modern Landscapes for Living,* Berkeley, Los Angeles & London: University of California Press, 1997.

Uide, A. "Greenhouse Effect." U.K.: *The Architectural Review,* May, 1998. (Greenhouse and park, Terrasson - Lavilledieu, Dordogne).

van de Kaa, Romke. "Floating on Air." U.K.: *The Garden Illustrated,* Oct/Nov, 1995. (Ton ter Linden's Impressionistic Dutch Garden).

Walker, Peter. *Minimalist Gardens*. USA: Spacemaker Press, 1997.

Watson, James. "Color Celebration." USA: *Florida Home and Garden,* April, 1989. (Raymond Jungles, Tropical Garden Rooms).

Way, David, and Hanne Cannegieter. "The Art of Gardening." U.K.: *The Garden,* August 1995. (Ton ter Linden).

Webb, Michael and Francisco Ascenso Cerver. *Redesigning City Squares and Plazas*. USA: Hearst Books International for Arco (Spain), 1997.

Weilacher, Udo. *Between Landscape Architecture and Land Art*. Germany: Birkhauser, 1996.

Weschler, Lawrence. "When Fountainheads Collide." USA: *The New Yorker,* December 3, 1997. (Robert Irwin and Richard Meier tangle over the Getty Center's Garden).

Whitney Library of Design. *Desvigne & Dalnoky.* USA: Watson-Guptill Publications, 1997.

Wilson, Karen C. "Plenty of Merit" USA: *San Diego Union-Tribune,* November 16, 1997. (Douglas Reed Therapeutic Garden, Wellesley, MA.).

Wortz, Melinda. "Robert Irwin: Aesthetic of Context." USA: *Artforum,* November 1981.

Yoos, Jennifer. "Conversation with Vincent James, George Hargreaves and James Carpenter." (Dayton Residence). Japan: *Architecture and Urbanism, (A&U),* December, 1998.